150th ANNIVERSARY • LOS ANGELES PUBLIC LIBRARY

150

1872 • 2022

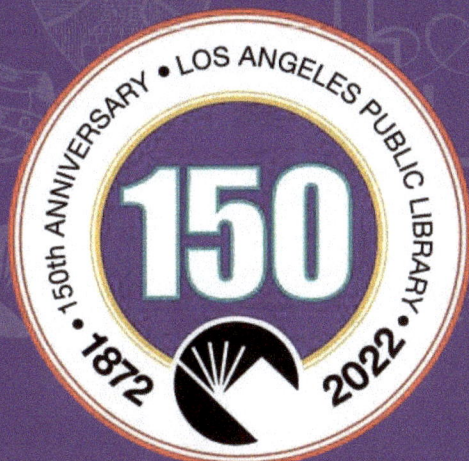

LAPL150
Our Story Is Yours

A Los Angeles Public Library
Sesquicentennial Celebration

Book and Exhibition Curated by
JAMES SHERMAN, Librarian, Literature & Fiction Department
& CHRISTINA RICE, Senior Librarian, Photo Collection

Text by JAMES SHERMAN

JOHN F. SZABO, City Librarian
KREN MALONE, Central Library Director

**LOS ANGELES
PUBLIC LIBRARY**

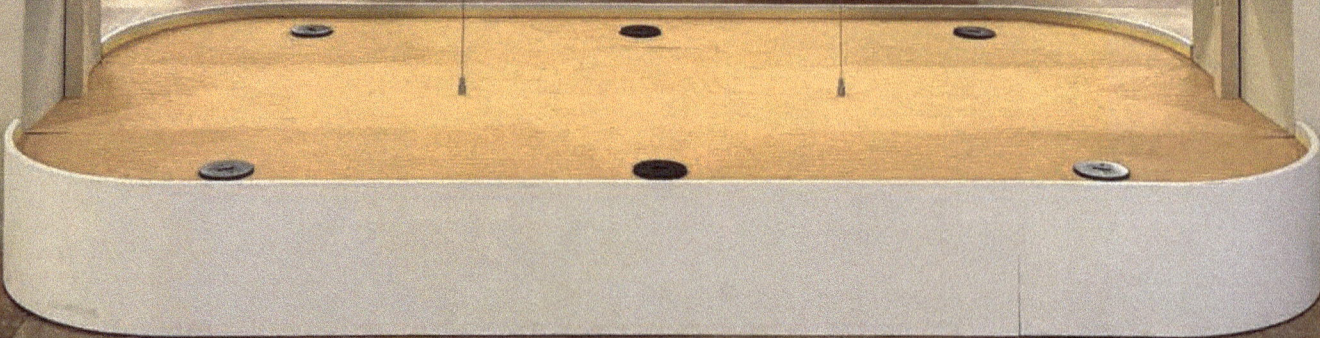

LITERATURE & FICTION

SCIENCE, TECHNOLOGY & PATENTS

ART, MUSIC & RECREATION

DIGITIZATION & SPECIAL COLLECTIONS

LOS ANGELES PUBLIC LIBRARY

PHOTO COLLECTION

SOCIAL SCIENCES, PHILOSOPHY & RELIGION

BUSINESS & ECONOMICS

HISTORY & GENEALOGY

POPULAR LIBRARY

TEEN'SCAPE

CHILDREN'S LITERATURE

INTERNATIONAL LANGUAGES

CONTENTS

OPPOSITE: **Central Library vinyl banner, 1993**
Institutional Archive, Special Collections
When the renovated and expanded Central Library reopened in October 1993, following a seven-year closure, the city celebrated in spectacular fashion. This is one of many banners that hung on the lampposts outside the building, signaling to residents that the doors of their beloved library were again open.

Central Library Department banners, 2023
Following the 1986 arson fires, the intact portion of the Central Library collection was temporarily relocated to the Title Insurance and Trust Building (also known as the Design Center of Los Angeles). These banners, listing the departments of the Central Library Services Division, are inspired by those that hung at the Spring Street location from 1989-1993. The patterns on these banners were largely modeled from the Art Deco ornamentation of Central Library's temporary home.

150th ANNIVERSARY • LOS ANGELES PUBLIC LIBRARY

150

1872 • 2022

Late in 1872, in a small but bustling pueblo of barely 6,000 people, something big was happening. A fire department and high school had just been founded, along with the first theater. Now the residents of El Pueblo de la Reina de los Ángeles knew what they wanted next for their town: a library. Two hundred citizens gathered to create the Los Angeles Library Association, which in 1878 would become the Los Angeles Public Library.

A spirit of civic pride and boosterism helped residents quickly achieve their immediate goal of having a place for the latest—though sometimes very late to arrive—newspapers and magazines from the distant east. The founders of the library had a more ambitious vision—to make a permanent public library from their fledgling organization lodged in rented rooms above one of the settlement's busiest saloons. Thus the light of learning was sparked and one of the oldest institutions of Los Angeles was born.

LAPL150
Our Story Is Yours

A Los Angeles Public Library
Sesquicentennial Celebration

Population soared over the next fifty years as the City of Los Angeles grew at record rates—to a half million in 1920 and to over a million by 1930. During the same period, the Los Angeles Public Library grew, from a mere 750 donated books at its founding, to the highest circulation of any public library in the country by 1933. Through boom times and setbacks, the Los Angeles Public Library reflected this enormous expansion, ever eager to keep pace with, yet often struggling to match, the City's dynamic development. One of the shining constants of Los Angeles Public Library's history is the dedicated service to its community that the Library has provided and continues to provide. The Library offers a place of opportunity for everyone, and has flourished largely because of the community's committed support, both politically and, significantly, through the crucial work of volunteers.

Los Angeles and its Library grew up together. **LAPL 150—Our Story Is Yours: A Los Angeles Public Library Sesquicentennial Celebration** is dedicated to the people of Los Angeles, and celebrates the story of our city through the Library's unique lens. While the Library's history is too expansive and complex to cover comprehensively in a single exhibit, we have highlighted some of the key aspects of the changing face of the Los Angeles Library System. How have the Library's collections, services and programs served the people of Los Angeles? How has the Library evolved to serve communities, and how have those communities helped the Library to grow? How has the Los Angeles Public Library continued to represent the democratic values of public libraries, providing free and open access to resources for life-long learning, and a commitment to equitable service for all?

Public Art

Various Branch Libraries, 2019
Gary Leonard, Institutional Collection

Public art has long been a component of Los Angeles Public Library locations and is now a requirement for all municipal buildings under the City of Los Angeles Public Works Improvements Arts Program. How many of these works do you recognize?

Platt

Mid-Valley

Memorial

Felipe de Neve

Memorial

Studio City

Canoga Park

Sun Valley

Ascot

Lake View Terrace

Lincoln Heights

North Hollywood

Fairfax

Sunland-Tujunga

Exposition Park

Jefferson

Little Tokyo

Malabar

John Muir

John C. Fremont

Northridge

Fairfax

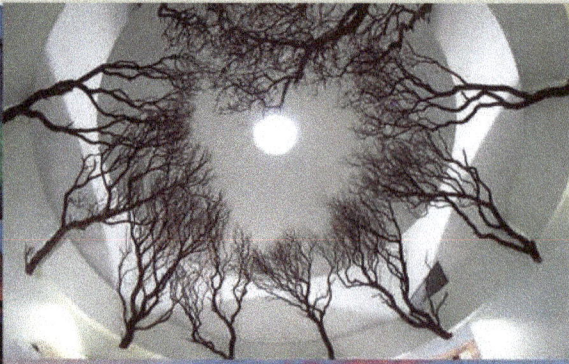

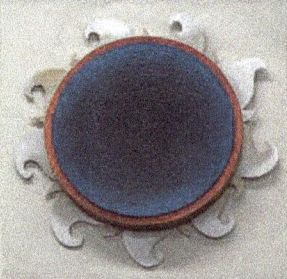

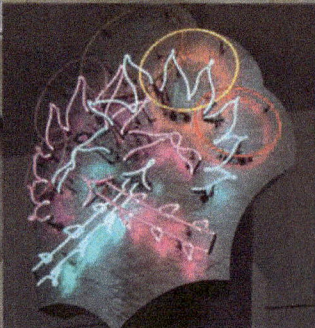

Valley Plaza	Mark Twain	Los Feliz		Washington Irving	Memorial	Arroyo Seco
Pio Pico-Koreatown	John C. Fremont	Pacoima		Los Feliz	West Valley	Atwater
Malabar	Jefferson	Palms-Rancho Park	Lincoln Heights		Valley Plaza	East Valley
Encino-Tarzana	Pico Union	Studio City		Venice	Memorial	Goldwyn Hollywood
Pio Pico-Koreatown	Baldwin Hills	El Sereno		Malabar	R.L. Stevenson	Lake View Terrace
Cahuenga	Ascot	Hyde Park		Cahuenga	Vernon	

We Need a Library

Clipping announcing meeting
to form a Library Association,
December 5, 1872
Los Angeles Daily Star

Clipping calling for the formation
of a Library Association,
November 30, 1872
Los Angeles Daily News

"We Need a Library!"
October 4, 1871
Los Angeles Daily Star

In 1872 Los Angeles was a town of about 6,000, yet was still the largest settlement in Southern California. From these very humble beginnings, the Los Angeles Public Library was born. Civic boosters, who believed that a library was essential to a town with big ambitions, formed the Los Angeles Library Association, with the intention of starting a full-fledged library. Slowly the Library Association became part of the City government. In 1878 administration and management was taken over by the City Council, and the Library Association was renamed the Los Angeles Public Library. The City Charter, established in 1889, assured funding and established a Board of Library Commissioners, which continues governance of the Library to this day.

First library location was two rooms in the Downey Block , located at Main and Temple Streets (1872-1889)
Security Pacific National Bank Collection

Reading room in Los Angeles City Hall, located at 226 South Broadway (1889-1906)
Herald Examiner Collection

The early years were marked by valiant yet futile attempts to keep up with the skyrocketing growth of Los Angeles, as the Library rented quarters that it quickly outgrew.

Rooftop reading room and smoking area at Homer Laughlin Building, located at 315 S. Broadway (1906-1908)
Institutional Collection

Reference Department in the Hamburger Department Store,
located at 8th and Hill Streets, and Broadway (1908-1914)
Institutional Collection

Interior of the Library at the Metropolitan Building, located at 315 West 5th Street (1914-1926)
Legacy Collection

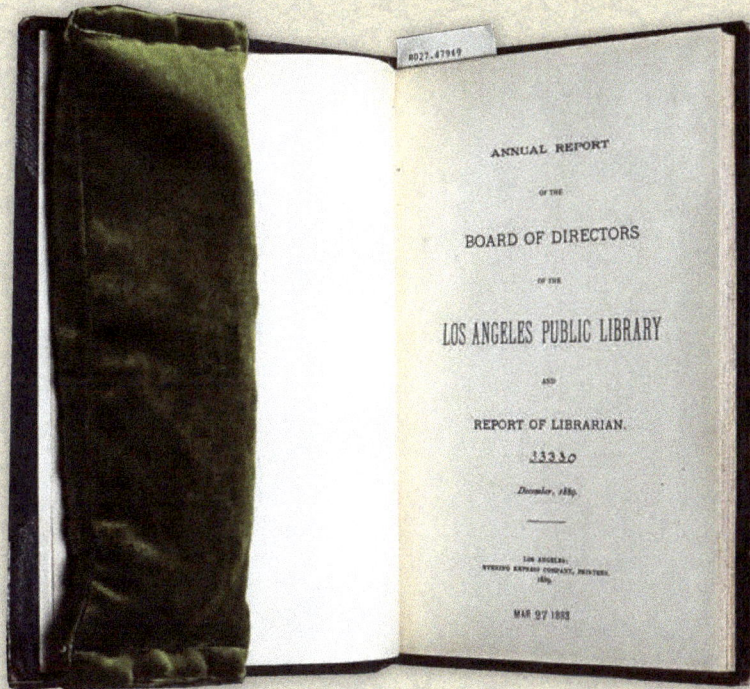

Annual Report of the Board of Directors
of the Los Angeles Public Library
and Report of Librarian, 1889
Special Collections

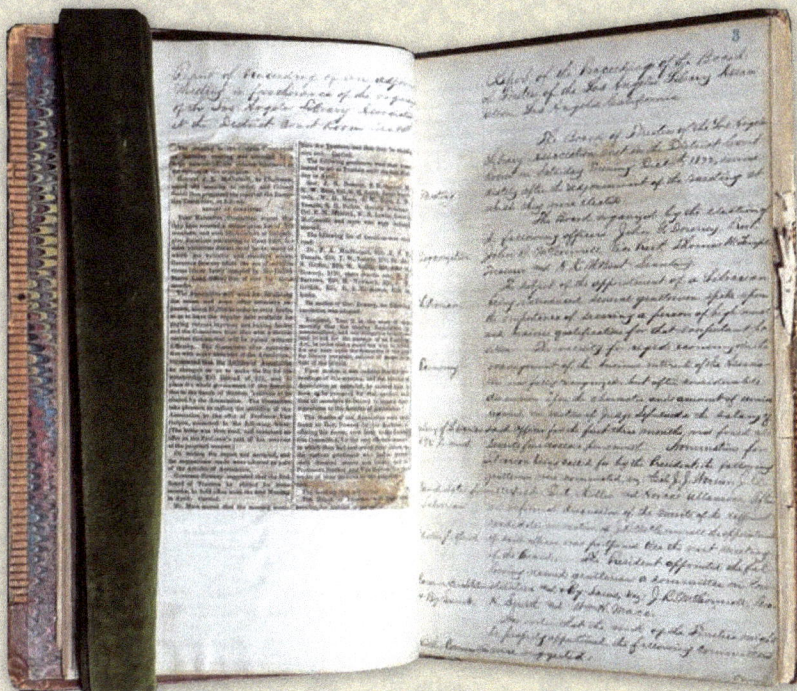

Los Angeles Public Library Minutes 1
1872-1889, creation of the
Los Angeles Library Association, 1872
Institutional Archive, Special Collections

Founding Documents

The Los Angeles Library Association was founded in 1872, enshrined in the meeting minutes found here. By the end of the decade, the small organization was adopted by the City government. The City Charter of 1889 included an article addressing the Library, within which its funding and its new governance by a Library Board were detailed.

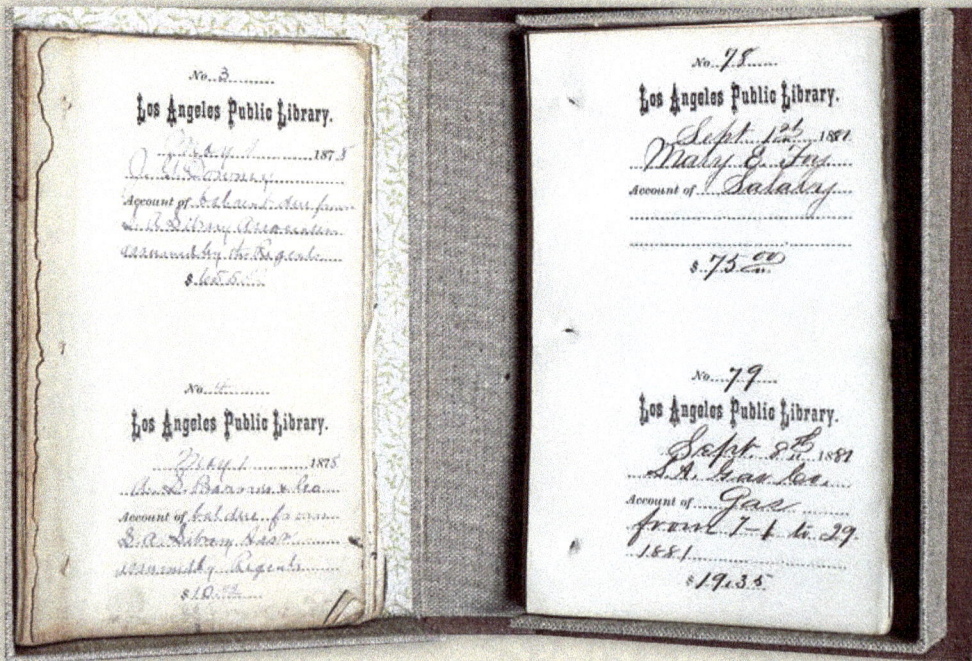

Accounting ledger showing rent payment to J.G. Downey, 1878, and City Librarian Mary Foy's salary, 1881
Institutional Archive, Special Collection

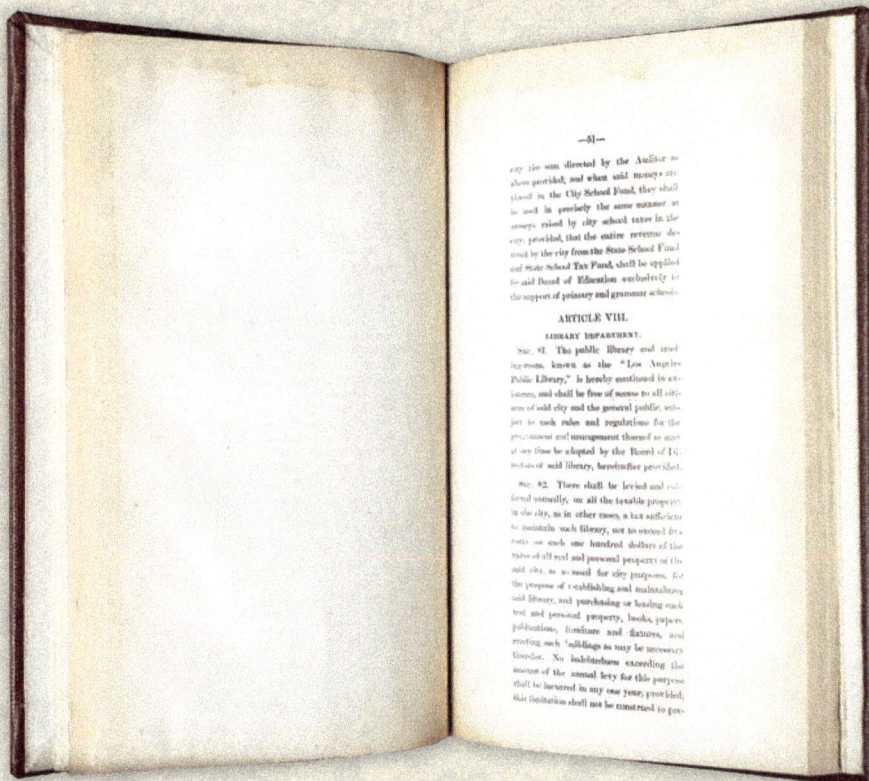

Charter of the City of Los Angeles, 1889
Special Collections

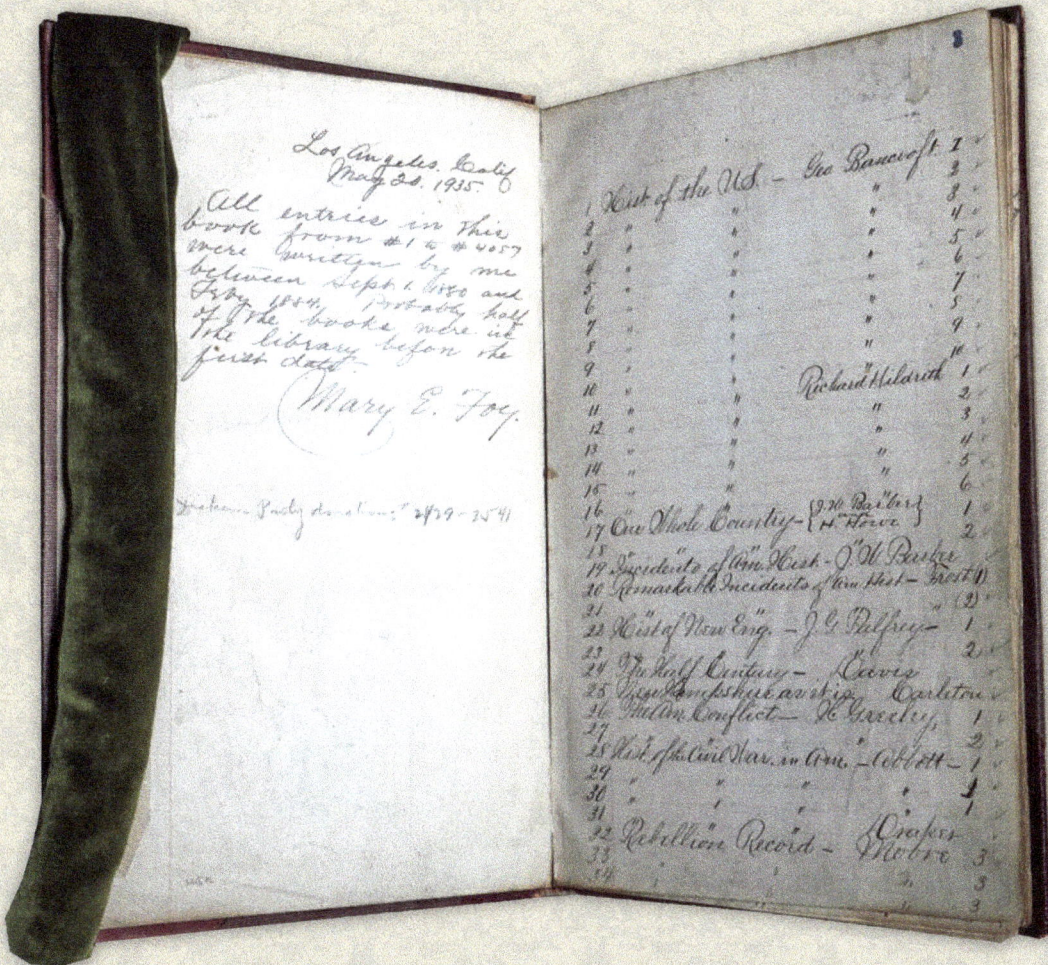

Book accession log in Mary Foy's handwriting, 1880-1888
Institutional Archive, Special Collections

Forming a Branch System

This adobe on Castelar Street, in the neighborhood known as Sonoratown,
was an early location of a satellite library
C.C. Pierce, Security Pacific National Bank Collection

Reading room of Dayton Library Station in the Cypress Park neighborhood, undated
Institutional Collection

To relieve crowding at the Library and to service neighborhoods new and old, the Los Angeles Public Library considered extending service to outside locations. The Library was already providing most of the books used in the Los Angeles schools, so they experimented with adapting this service to deliver books to different locations in various neighborhoods. Sometimes they would establish Delivery Stations, which were semi-permanent locations with part-time Library employees, such as at Settlement Houses and Fire Stations.

Mission Acres Library Station in the San Fernando Valley, undated
Institutional Collection

Other locations, known as Deposit Stations, were volunteer attempts to 'audition' a community space that would be a candidate to join the Los Angeles Public Library system on a more permanent basis. These were located in retail or institutional spaces, such as drug stores and neighborhood club houses. Volunteers would manage a small collection of donated books, with occasional pick-up and delivery of Library books. If the Deposit Station enjoyed sustained popular use, the Library would arrange an extended loan of the books to the location for their community members, and if success continued, the Deposit Station would become a Delivery Station and eventually a branch library.

Echo Park Playground Branch Library, circa 1924
Legacy Collection

Atwater Station, located at the Atwater Avenue School, circa 1924
Legacy Collection

San Pedro Branch Library (annexed Carnegie), circa 1906
Legacy Collection

Cahuenga Branch Library (original Carnegie), undated. Still in operation
Legacy Collection

The first freestanding permanent locations were made possible through a gift from Andrew Carnegie, the steel magnate, who provided funding to build libraries across the United States. In total, the Library system had ten Carnegie Libraries: six Carnegie buildings were constructed for the Los Angeles Public Library (three of these are still in use) and four were added by annexation.

Watts Branch Library (annexed Carnegie), 1945
Institutional Collection

Hollywood Branch Library (annexed Carnegie), circa 1912
Institutional Collection

The Carnegies were both a source of pride and a spur to gather support for a larger network that could better serve the rapidly expanding city. Thanks to a popular bond issue in 1921 the Library finally obtained funds for a permanent Central Building and eleven new branches; a follow-up bond in 1925 would add 14 more. The Los Angeles Public Library was finally established as a serious metropolitan system.

Vernon Branch Library (original Carnegie), undated
Institutional Collection

Eagle Rock Branch Library (annexed Carnegie), undated
Institutional Collection

Lincoln Heights Branch Library (original Carnegie), undated. Still in operation
Institutional Collection

Vermont Square Branch Library (original Carnegie), undated. Still in operation
Institutional Collection

Arroyo Seco Branch Library (original Carnegie), 1945
Legacy Collection

Boyle Heights Branch Library (original Carnegie), undated
Institutional Collection

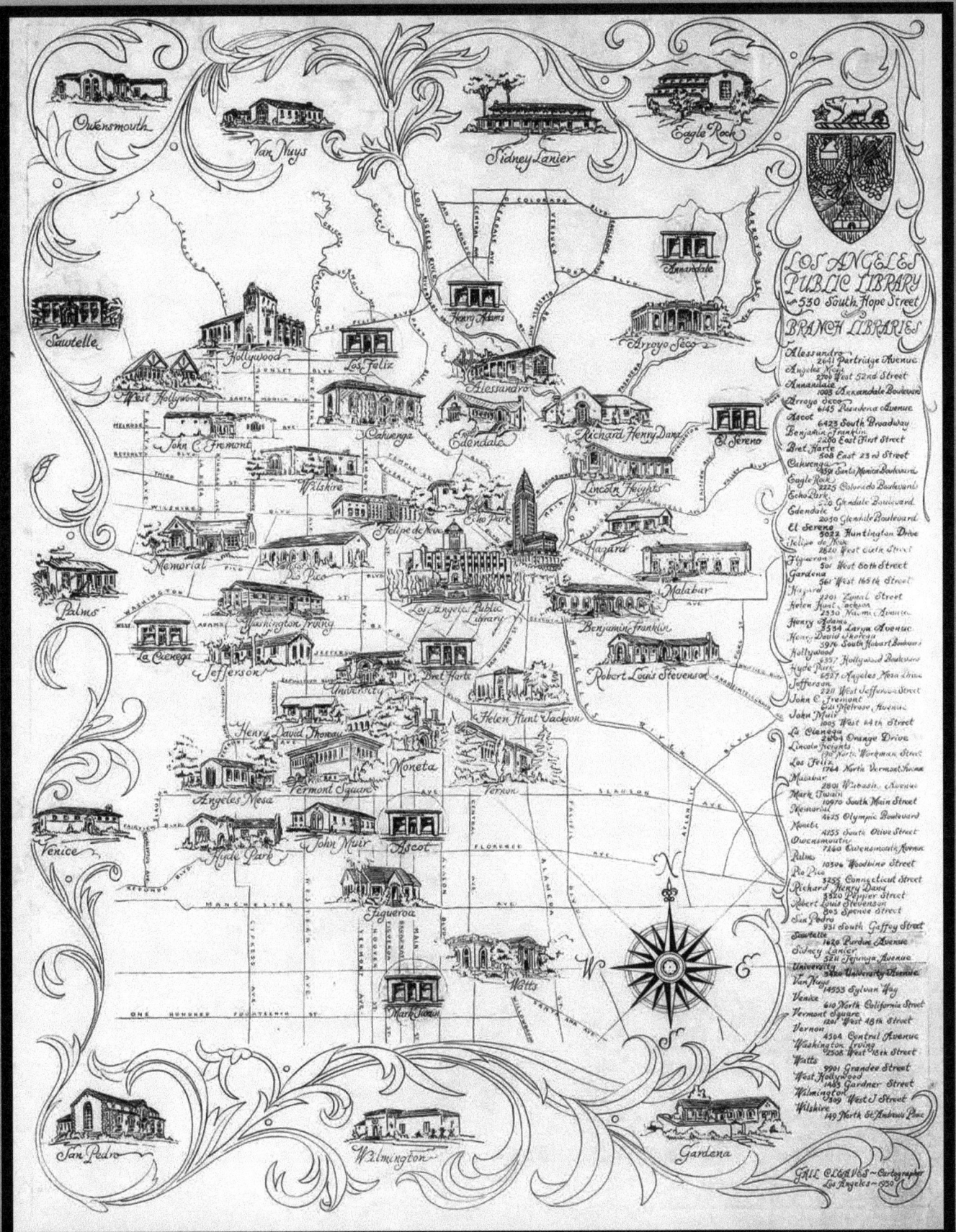

Map of Los Angeles Public Library branches, painted by Gail Cleaves,
formerly mounted just inside the 5th Street entrance to Central Library, 1930

**Library School of the
Los Angeles Public Library**

This is to certify that

Hilda Judith Rothstein

*having completed in a satisfactory manner the
course of study prescribed for graduation from
this school is hereby awarded this Diploma.*

*Given at Los Angeles, California on the 30th
day of June in the year 1931*

Faith E. Smith
Principal of the Library School

Orra E. Monnette
President of the Board of Library Directors

Everett R. Perry
Librarian

LEFT: **Library School of the Los Angeles
Public Library diploma, 1931**
Institutional Archive,
Special Collections

BELOW: **Library School of the
Los Angeles Public Library course
catalog, 1916 & 1919-1920**
Institutional Archive,
Special Collections

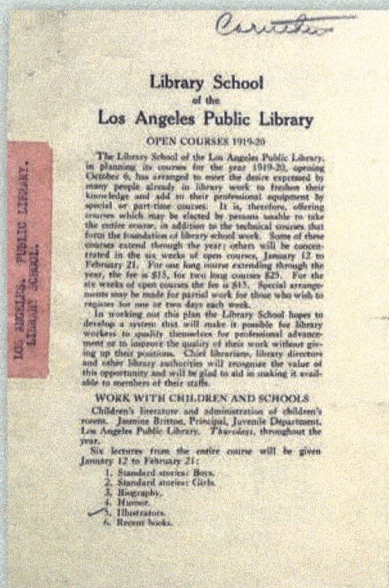

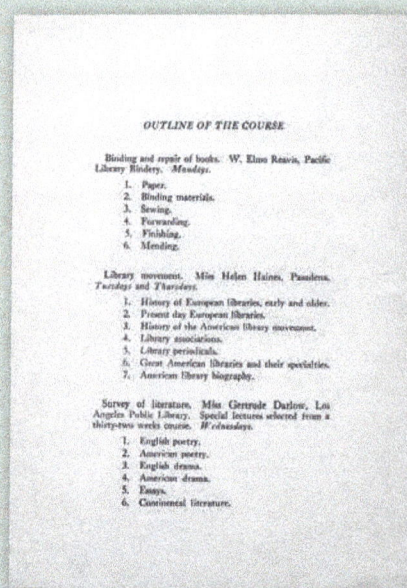

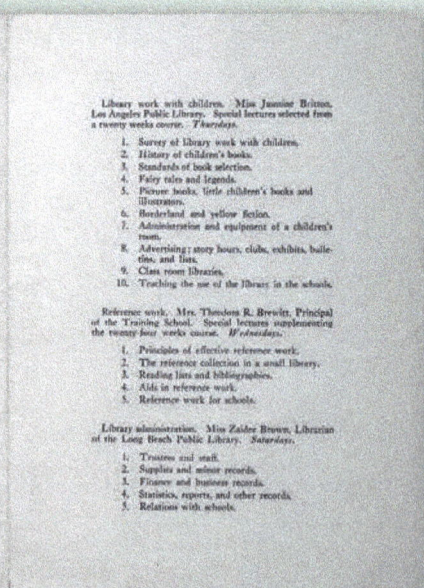

Library School of the Los Angeles Public Library, 1891-1932

The Los Angeles Public Library was one of the first public libraries to establish a defined system of professional instruction. Beginning as a basic training course with six students, by 1914 it was a one-year library school with a curriculum that included book selection, children's services, and library administration. More than 600 graduates influenced professional standards nationwide and beyond — in 1912 the school assisted Shaniavsky University (Moscow) in designing the first training program for librarians in Russia. The Library School was an unfortunate victim of the Great Depression — in 1932 the school was assimilated into USC's recently established School of Library Service.

[FORM 1.]

No. 135, Nov. 91.

APPLICATION FOR POSITION AS LIBRARY PUPIL.

To the Board of Directors of the Los Angeles Public Library:

I hereby make application to be placed on the list for appointment as a pupil in the PUBLIC LIBRARY, subject to existing rules and any rules to be hereafter made by the Board of Directors, and I herewith furnish answers to the questions below, in my own handwriting.

QUESTIONS:	ANSWERS.
1. Give full name.	
2. Residence (street and number).	
3. How long have you resided in Los Angeles?	
4. Place of birth.	
5. Age.	
6. Are you engaged in any occupation? Give particulars.	
7. What school training and business experience, if any, have you had?	
8. Have you a father living? If so, state where and in what business.	
9. Have you a mother living?	
10. Do you reside with your parents?	
11. What is the condition of your general health?	
12. Have you read the printed rules and regulations of the Library?	
13. Have you any knowledge of languages?	
14. Give names and address of at least two persons to whom you refer.	

Signature of Applicant,

Dated

Note: Applications must be from young women not under seventeen years of age, and actual residents of the city. They must agree to give three hours a day service for a period of at least six months, at the end of which time, upon passing an examination satisfactorily to the board, they will be placed upon the substitute list for paid employment as opportunity offers.

4   5

Booklet with facsimile
of Library School
application
Institutional Archive,
Special Collections

Library School
OF THE
Los Angeles Public Library

(Member Association of American Library Schools)

The Library School of the Los Angeles Public Library offers two courses, one of nine months which prepares for any type of library work, and one of two months which prepares for the position of junior attendant in the Los Angeles Public Library. The school is the outgrowth of a practical course of training for library workers conducted by the Los Angeles Public Library since 1891. It has grown from an apprentice class to a library school giving the standard one year library school course, in which the technical subjects are taught, and elective courses in library work with children, high school library work and bibliographical cataloging are offered.

ENTRANCE REQUIREMENTS
Senior Course

Age. Applicants must be over twenty and under thirty-five years of age, except in the case of persons who have had considerable previous library experience or other special qualifications.

Education. As a good education is an essential foundation for library work, no applicants are accepted who have not completed at least three years of college work or a satisfactory equivalent in library experience. A knowledge of literature, history, economics, sociology and modern languages, especially French, German and Spanish, makes the best preparation for library work.

Entrance Examination. All candidates who are not college graduates must pass an entrance examination in literature, history, current events, and general information, and in sight translation of one modern language, which may be French, German or Spanish, as preferred.

Junior Course

Age. Applicants must be over eighteen and under thirty-five years, except in the cases of persons who have had previous library experience.

Library School pamphlet
detailing admission
requirements,
Institutional Archive,
Special Collections

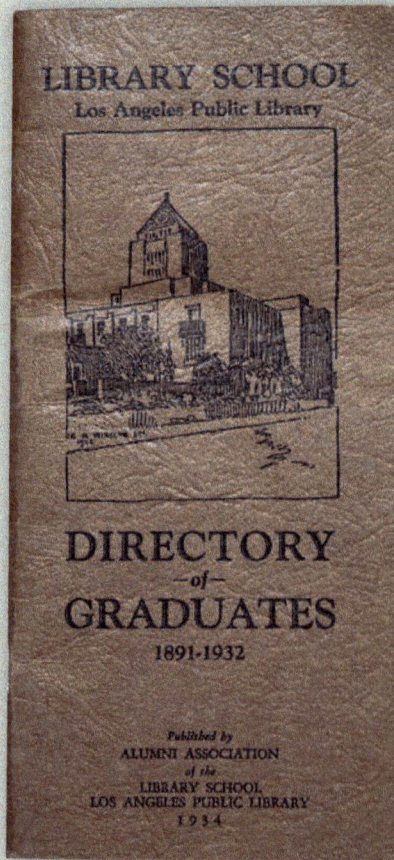

Library School,
Directory of Graduates, 1934
Institutional Archive,
Special Collections

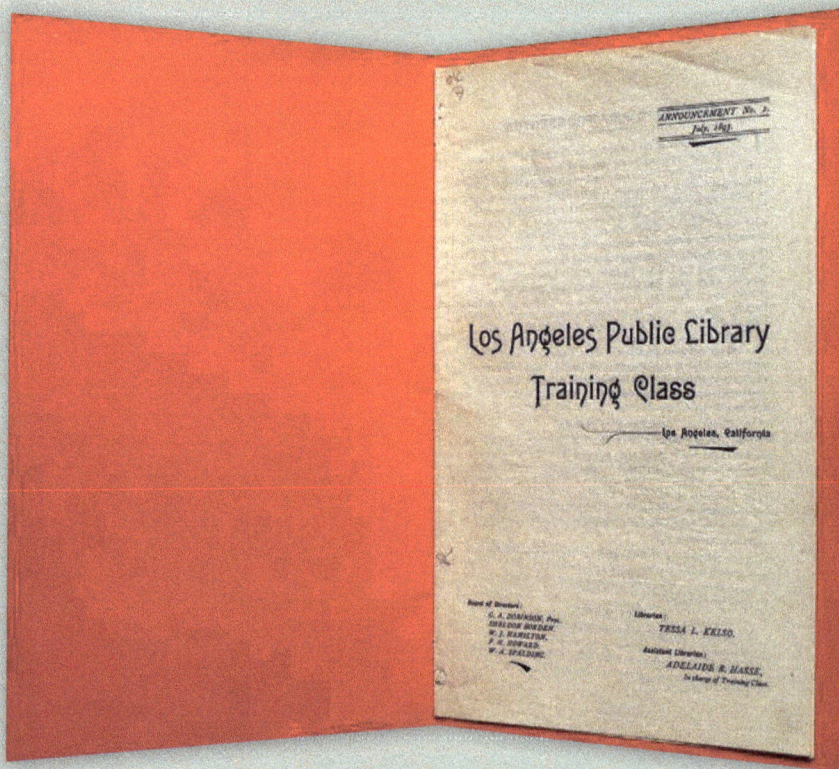

Los Angeles Public Library Training Class, Announcement No. 1, 1893
Institutional Archive,
Special Collections

Los Angeles Public Library School class photo
Institutional Archive, Special Collections

Librarians Affiliate With Alumni Association

Alumni of Los Angeles Public Library School, Now Incorporated into the University Curriculum, Become Eligible for General Association Membership

AN OUTSTANDING RECORD of forty-one years of library training was concluded in June, 1932, when the Library School of the Los Angeles Public Library was discontinued. During twenty-three years as a training class and eighteen years as a standard one-year library school, 635 students received diplomas.

Of this total, 345 are at present in varied fields of library service. Ten alumni are directors of municipal libraries, seven of county libraries, and four of college libraries. Other graduates are also placed in a multiplicity of important book business positions.

With the termination of the Public Library School as an independent institution four years ago, the University of Southern California later incorporated its classes into the University curriculum. On the 14th of last month, graduates of the Los Angeles library school were welcomed into Troy's General Alumni Association at a dinner which occurred in the Foyer of Town and Gown on campus.

The visitors at the affair were received by Dr. Carl Howson, president-elect of the S.C. graduate group.

Miss Reba Dwight, prexy of the original library school's alumni, then introduced Miss Helen Haines, who served on the faculty of that institution for fourteen years. Miss Haines briefed the history of the Los Angeles Public Library School since its inception in 1891 to the date of its close in 1932. In addition, the former library school teacher outlined the opening of the School of Library Service at the University of Southern California. To quote Miss Haines's speech:

"From the Los Angeles Library School during those years of its existence a vitalizing current has flowed through southern California. It has not been held within sectional boundaries; but its most invigorating and widest influence has been within our own region—in the preponderant de-

Miss Helen Haines
"14 years of library school service"

Below: Main Entrance Doheny Library.

... by ...
JOHNS HARRINGTON '39

velopment and activity of the public libraries in the southern part of the state; in the growth of expert library work for children, stemming largely from the training first available here; in the increasing volume and effectiveness of school library work, through the whole educational system."

The last director of the library school when it was affiliated with the Public Library, Miss Faith Smith spoke to the dinner guests about the organization of the school at S.C. last September. Expressing her desire for the success of the new curriculum at Troy, Miss Smith commented: "May this new school cement the bond between universities and libraries in this community, both types of institutions working for the advancement and diffusion of knowledge and understanding among the people of the community."

President-elect Howson of the S.C. alumni association introduced other notable librarians present at the gathering, including Miss Christian R. Dick, librarian of the University; Dr. Andrew D. Osborne, Director of the School of Library Service; Miss Opal Stone, instructor in the Library School at S.C.; Miss Marion Horton and Mrs. Theodore R. Brewitt, past directors of the Los Angeles Public Library School.

A highlight on the evening's program was the reading by Dr. Frank C. Baxter of the S.C. Department of English of his well-known "lost chapter" of *Alice In Wonderland*. The white rabbit of the story was a librarian who kept repeating the eternal excuse of every librarian since his institution's founding, "It's at the binder's! It's at the binder's!"

Authors were divided into three classes in Dr. Baxter's "lost chapter":

"Art for art's sake!"
"Art, for God's sake!"
"Art, for cryin' out loud!"

Alice thought it was all very silly.

PAGE SEVENTEEN

Library School Alumni Association article
Institutional Archive, Special Collections

Ups and Downs

Children illustrate book languages available from the Library, 1928
Eyre Powell Chamber of Commerce Collection

Long circulation line, 1931
Herald Examiner Collection

The Library was an essential part of metropolitan life, whose resources and staff met the needs of the growing city and changing demographics, including collections in many languages. It also became the focal point of community activities and provided neighborhood gathering spaces.

TEN YEARS OF UPS AND DOWNS
IN LIBRARY USE AND INCOME

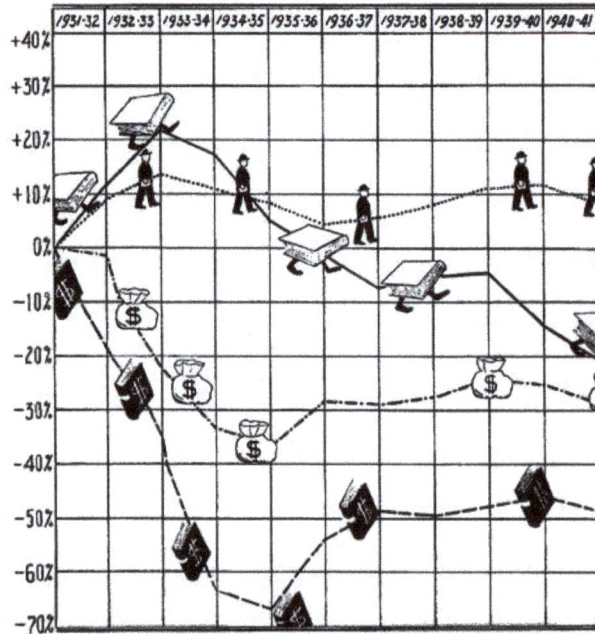

	1931-32	1932-33	1933-34	1934-35	1935-36	1936-37	1937-38	1938-39	1939-40	1940-41
+40%										
+30%										
+20%										
+10%										
0%										
-10%										
-20%										
-30%										
-40%										
-50%										
-60%										
-70%										

CERTIFICATE OF

Recognition

AWARDED TO Staff of the Los Angeles Public Library

IN APPRECIATION OF YOUR FAITHFUL AND UNTIRING SERVICE TO MEN AND WOMEN IN THE ARMED FORCES WHO, THANKS TO YOUR KINDLY ATTITUDE AND GENEROUS HOSPITALITY, CARRY WITH THEM TO THE FAR CORNERS OF THE EARTH MEMORIES OF HAPPY HOURS SPENT IN OUR U.S.O. CLUBS AND IN YOUR HOMES.

LOS ANGELES AREA U.S.O. BOARD

CHAIRMAN
COMMITTEE CHAIRMAN
DIRECTOR

Nov. 22 1944
DATE

USO Certificate of Recognition, 1944
Institutional Collection, Special Collections

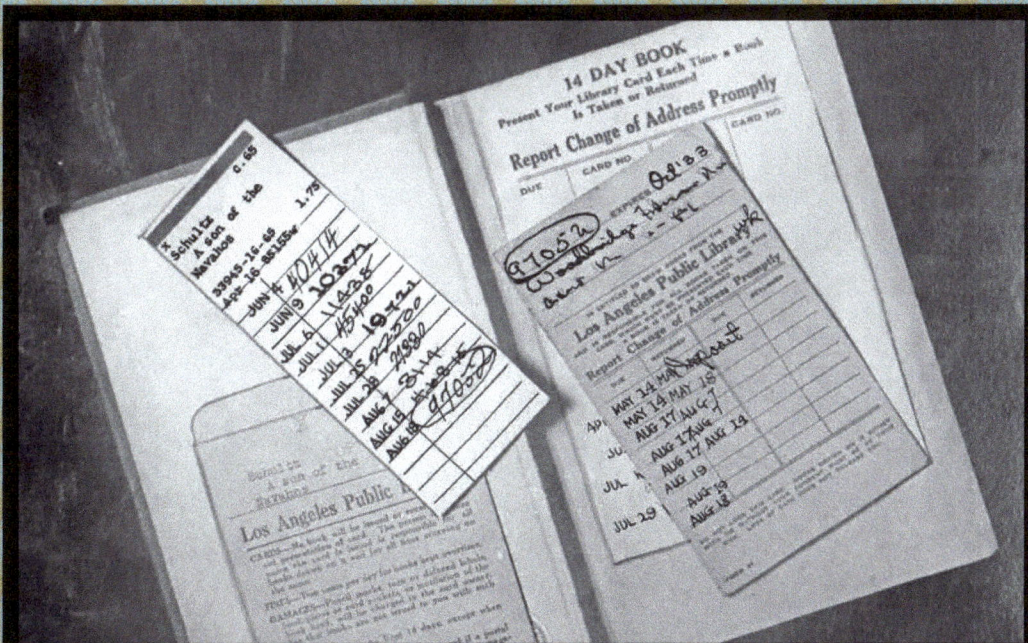

Self-service system instituted to help alleviate long circulation lines, 1931
Herald Examiner Collection

Easter story hour at Vermont Square Branch Library, 1931
Institutional Collection

The Library's importance to the community was most evident during the Great Depression. It was the place for education, job searches, and entertainment, and the public flocked through the door in droves, so much so that there were queues for people to come inside. In 1933, at the lowest part of the depression, the Los Angeles Public Library boasted the highest circulation of any library system in the nation.

Circulation Department, 1935
Institutional Collection

Spirituals program at Malabar Branch Library, 1933
Institutional Collection

Sign on the Figueroa Branch Library signaling its permanent closure due to budget cuts, 1941
Legacy Collection

Yet the Depression eventually took its toll on the Library. The number of people coming to Southern California didn't decrease, but the funds to support the Los Angeles Public Library did. Due to large budget shortfalls, the Library was forced to lay off staff and close some of its branches, further reducing public services.

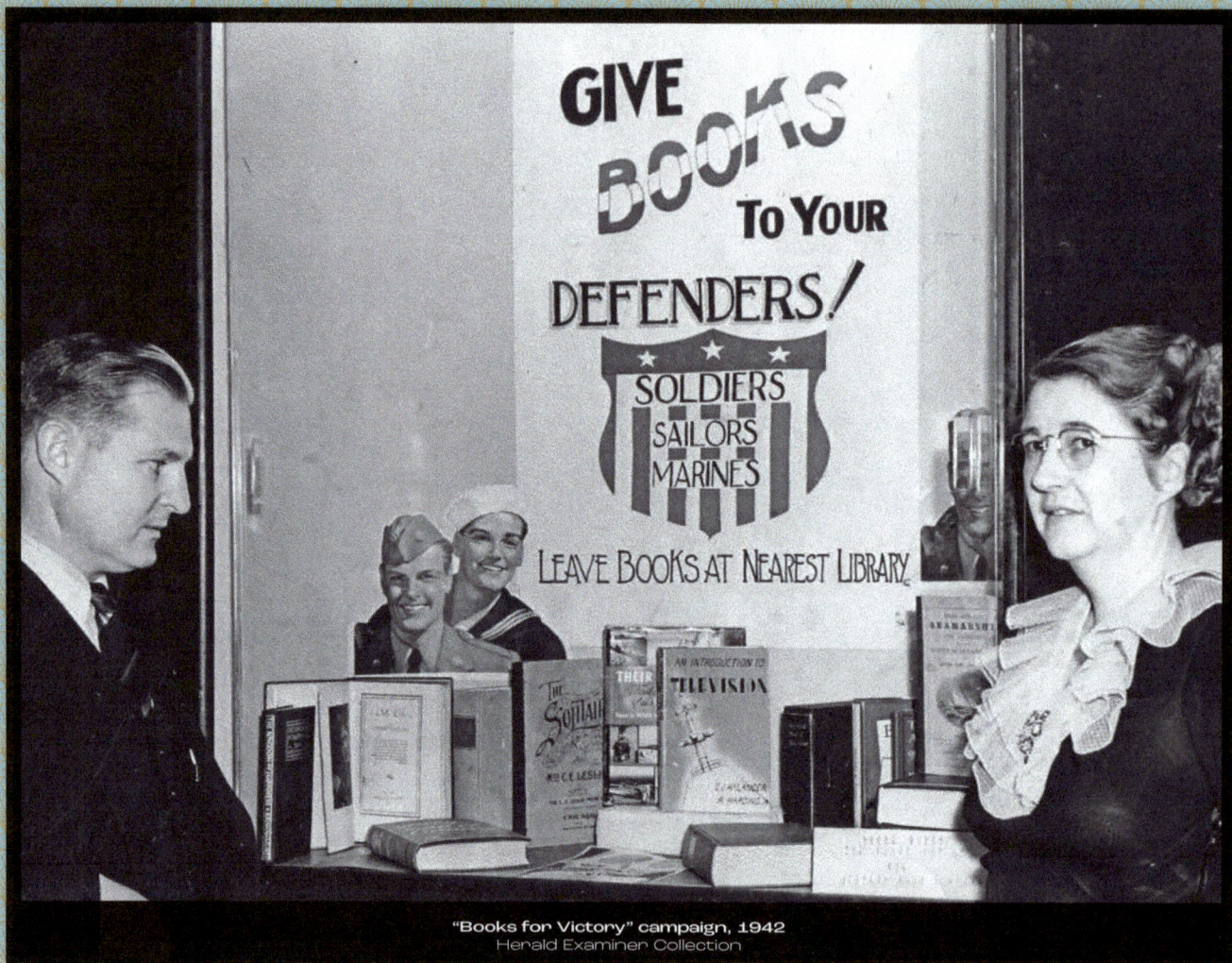

"Books for Victory" campaign, 1942
Herald Examiner Collection

World War II followed on the heels of the Great Depression. The Library did its part in the war effort. Many library staff joined up, and those on the home front worked hard to provide books for the military and the Merchant Marine.

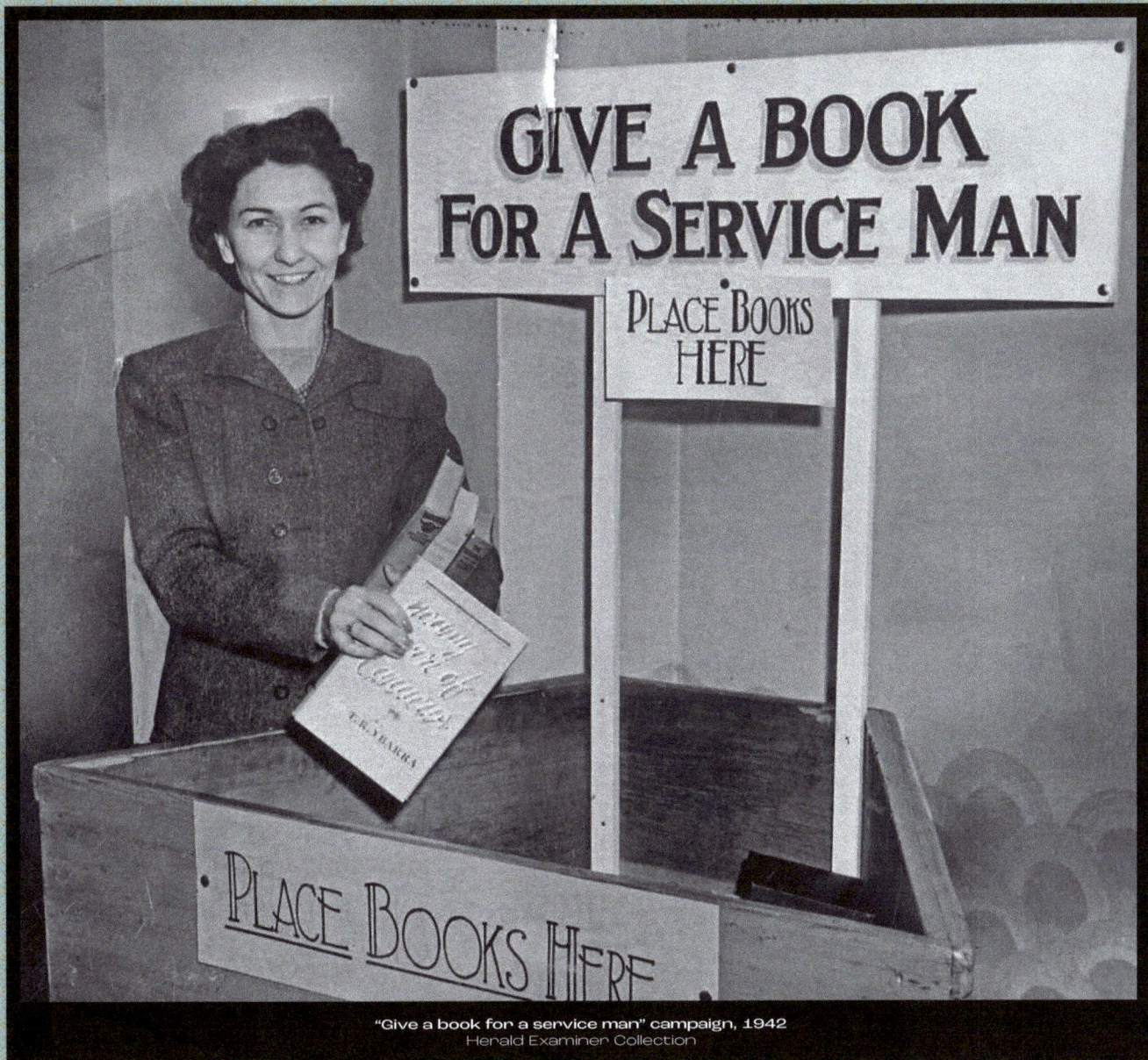

GIVE A BOOK
FOR A SERVICE MAN

PLACE BOOKS
HERE

PLACE BOOKS HERE

"Give a book for a service man" campaign, 1942
Herald Examiner Collection

American Library Association Convention in Los Angeles, 1930
Eyre Powell Chamber of Commerce Collection

1930 American Library Association Conference

Los Angeles' growing importance as a major metropolitan region was demonstrated when it hosted the 52nd Annual Convention of the American Library Association (ALA). Two thousand librarians from across the United States, as well as from Canada, Mexico, and parts of Europe, attended the event held at Central Library and the neighboring Biltmore Hotel. According to City Librarian Everett R. Perry who, with Los Angeles Public Library staff, organized the event, "Los Angeles was selected as the convention city because of its rapid development into a world literary center."

Author and Newbery Award winner Rachel Field is shown aboard an airliner
during an ALA conference publicity stunt, 1930
Eyre Powell Chamber of Commerce Collection

American Library Association Conference registration package materials, 1930
Donation of Helene Mochedlover, Institutional Archive, Special Collections

A Tale of Two Cities

Surveying land for Encino-Tarzana Branch Library, 1960
Jon Woods, Valley Times Collection

Groundbreaking for North Hollywood Branch Library expansion, 1956
Valley Times Collection

Having weathered the storms of the Great Depression and World War II, the economy of Southern California enjoyed a postwar boom. The resulting population explosion created the need for many more library locations to service the expanding city. A bond in 1959 saw many new branches built across Los Angeles, focusing on the areas of most rapid growth, primarily in the San Fernando Valley.

Sun Valley Branch Library groundbreaking, 1961
Jon Woods, Valley Times Collection

Vanowen Branch Library (now Valley Plaza Branch Library) groundbreaking, 1961
Valley Times Collection

Studio City Branch Library groundbreaking, 1962
Jeff Goldwater, Valley Times Collection

Artists' conception of the new Baldwin Hills Branch Library,
designed by the architectural firm of Hunter & Benedict, A.I.A. of Los Angeles, 1960
Institutional Archive, Special Collections

Artists' conception of the new Encino-Tarzana Branch Library,
designed by the architectural firm of Rochlin & Baran, circa 1960
Institutional Archive, Special Collections

Northridge Branch Library groundbreaking, 1962
Gordon Dean, Valley Times Collection

Sherman Oaks Branch Library groundbreaking, 1961
Valley Times Collection

Baldwin Hills Branch Library groundbreaking, 1960
Institutional Collection

Loyola Village Branch Library groundbreaking, 1960
Institutional Collection

The 1960s in L.A. is the tale of two cities. In one part of Los Angeles, tract homes and suburbs grew with a new middle class. Smaller communities that once had been served, if at all, by a constellation of the temporary delivery stations, became the setting for the groundbreaking of many new branch libraries.

Palisades Branch Library groundbreaking, 1962
Institutional Collection

Fairfax Branch Library groundbreaking, 1962
Institutional Collection

Palms Rancho Branch Library groundbreaking, 1963
Institutional Collection

Mar Vista Branch Library groundbreaking, 1961
Institutional Collection

HOW THINGS HAVE CHANGED IN THE LAST 10 YEARS

	1945	1955
Population served (est.)	1,749,000	2,201,000
Books in the library	1,706,615	2,210,616
Branch libraries	40	52
Part-time stations	57	0
Bookmobiles	0	4
Bookmobile stops	0	52
Number of people holding library cards	303,102	502,029
Books lent for home use in a year	6,309,823	9,254,546
Number of people viewing educational films	0	347,820
Dollars spent for year's operation	$1,144,250	$3,299,345
Employees	518	732
Annual salary of average employee	$ 1,713	$ 3,576

From *The Light of Learning, An Illustrated History of the Los Angeles Public Library*, 1993

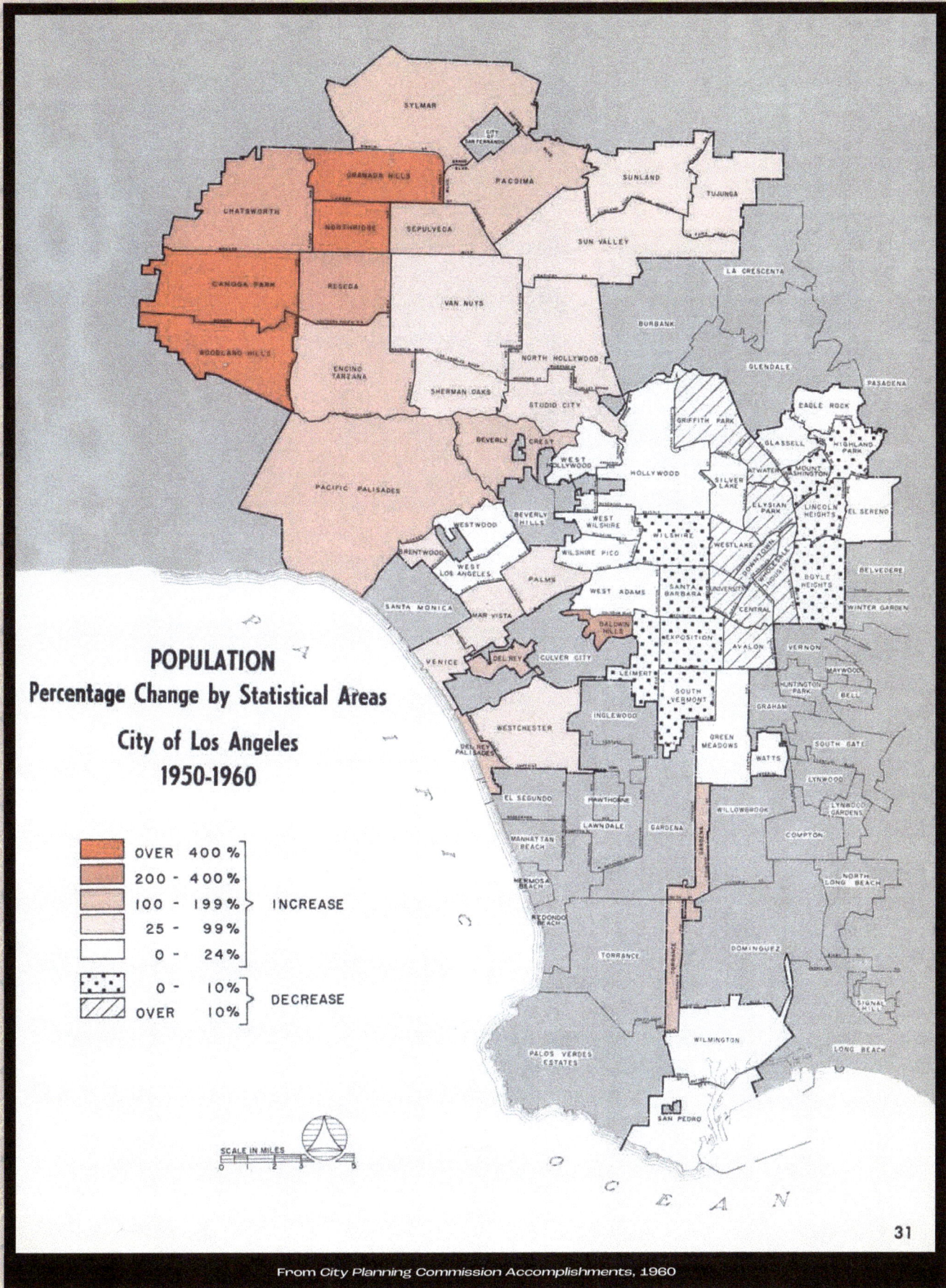

POPULATION
Percentage Change by Statistical Areas
City of Los Angeles
1950-1960

Legend:
- OVER 400%
- 200 - 400%
- 100 - 199% } INCREASE
- 25 - 99%
- 0 - 24%
- 0 - 10% } DECREASE
- OVER 10%

SCALE IN MILES
0 1 2 3 5

31

From *City Planning Commission Accomplishments*, 1960

But in the urban center, population was on the decline, a growing trend across the country, which further eroded older inner city communities. These conditions, coupled with the ongoing fight for Civil Rights, sparked further unrest, as seen in the Watts Uprisings. In response, the Los Angeles Public Library committed to improving civic and informational support for the city's diverse communities.

I'm BLACK and I'm proud!

Jack Sisson, Revolutionary War Hero

Had reason to be proud of his American heritage. He was one of several hundred Negroes who fought for American Independence during the Revolutionary War. Practically every regiment had Negroes serving as enlisted men, many of whom distinguished themselves in battle. They were usually found serving in the Continental line which formed the backbone of the American army.

LOS ANGELES PUBLIC LIBRARY - 1970

Booklist, circa 1970
Institutional Collection,
Special Collections

LA Library

Slates fall programs on Mexican Americans

A series of three community programs discussing the history and culture of Mexican Americans will be conducted early this fall by the Los Angeles Public Library, it was announced this week by Mrs. Eileen Kenyon, president, Board of Library Commissioners.

"Emphasis: Americans of Mexican Descent," is the theme of the three programs scheduled by the library in September, October and November.

"This series will focus attention on the problems of Mexican Americans and, at the same time, exhibit and discuss this group's cultural heritage and contributions to America," said Mrs. Kenyon.

This is the second year of library-sponsored community programs discussing problems of minorities. In 1969, three programs, titled "Crisis: Black and White," were conducted.

The first program in the 1970 Emphasis series is scheduled for Sunday, September 13, at the Central Library, 630 West Fifth Street. Titled, "Mexican Americans, the Living Culture," the program will include a panel discussion on the cultural and artistic contributions of Mexicans and Mexican Americans. It will be accompanied by a large exhibit of local and Mexican art and artifacts, as well as continuous showings of films and filmstrips on the subject.

Two subsequent programs in October and November will discuss reading problems of Mexican Americans and current developments in the

"Chicano Movement."

"We hope to attract outstanding speakers at each of the three programs," said Mrs. Kenyon. "The programs will be conducted in an informal atmosphere to encourage participation in the discussion by those in attendance."

In conjunction with the Emphasis series, the Los Angeles Public Library is reinforcing its collection of library books and materials on Mexican American history at the Central Library and 61 branches. The Spanish language book collection will also be expanded to serve a wider range of readers.

Mrs. Kenyon noted that an estimated 500,000 Spanish surname persons reside in Southern California. Mexican Americans form the second largest minority group in the nation.

During the past year, several novels, non-fiction works and films have been produced on Mexican American history and culture. But, according to Mrs. Kenyon, there is still a definite lack of information and resource material on the subject.

"However, this is now slowly changing. Publishers, libraries, educational institutions and the public in general are becoming aware of the problems of Mexican Americans, and the demand for such information is being strongly felt," she said.

Hollywood Bowl

NOSOTROS hosts '

"Night of Stars in the Hollywood

The Cage'

Clipping highlighting series of programs titled,
"Emphasis: Americans of Mexican Descent," July 23, 1970
El Sereno Star

CRISIS: BLACK AND WHITE

Discussion Due On Racism

"Crisis: Black and White" is the subject of the Los Angeles Public Library's first Community Discussion Program, it was announced today by commission president Leontyne B. King.

Five distinguished speakers will appear in a panel discussion and community dialogue at the Central Library, 630 W. Fifth St., March 16, at 2 p.m. It will be the first of three programs scheduled throughout the year to help citizens gain a better understanding of the racial problems that have become a part of American life.

"We announced our Community Discussion Program during Negro History Week to emphasize the fact that this subject cannot be properly dealt with in a seven-day period," said Mrs. King. "The March 16 program will focus on Negro history with future programs centering on Negro culture and art and contemporary problems. The Los Angeles Public Library is saying through these programs that there is something ordinary citizens can do about the racial problem — they can open their minds to the information that is available."

The five speakers for the March 16 program are: Abdulhamid Akoni, coordinator of the Afro-American Studies Department, California State College at Los Angeles, and the founder of the First Moslem Mosque of Los Angeles; Louis Lomax, author, lecturer, journalist, TV personality and active civil rights worker; John Caughey, professor of history at UCLA and author of "Land of the Free," the controversial state approved textbook showing the involvement of minorities in the development of America; Joseph Boskin, USC history professor; and Charles Cline, chairman of the Education Committee of the Black Educators Association.

Clipping advertising "Crisis: Black and White," a community discussion at Central Library which had over 500 people in attendance,
March 14, 1969
Los Angeles Evening Citizen News

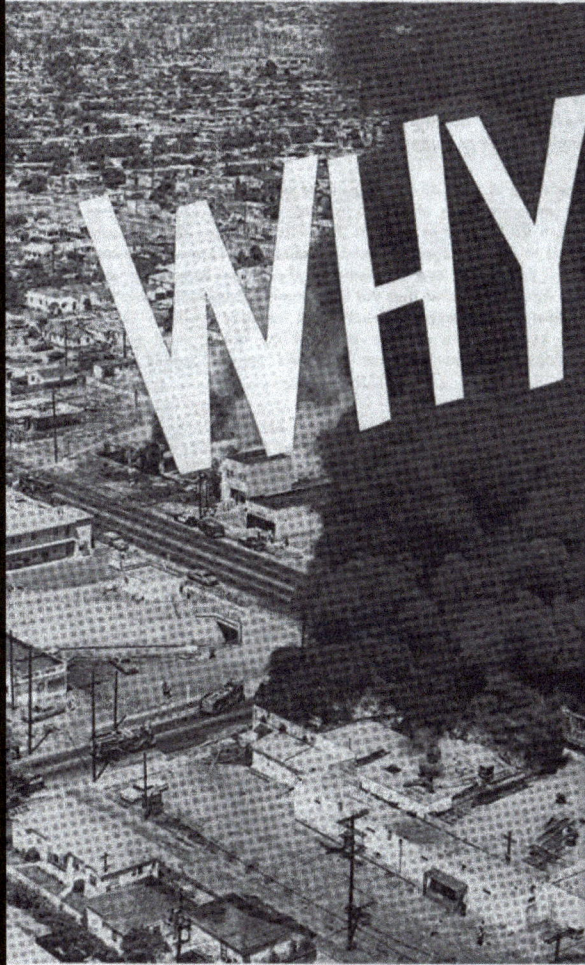

LOS ANGELES - AUGUST 1965

WHY

LOS ANGELES PUBLIC LIBRARY

As Los Angeles begins to heal the scars of the city's most disastrous riot thousands of citizens are asking each other WHY? State and local authorities will conduct extensive investigations probing the whys of this riot. Sociologists, economists and other professionals will study the Los Angeles riot and its causes for months and years to come. Answers are already being offered and there will be hundreds more before long. There will never be a single answer or explanation.

One thing is certain—the citizens of Los Angeles must acquire a better understanding of the social and economic problems that lie beneath the surface of this riot. The citizens of Los Angeles cannot afford to wait until careful and detailed studies are made and published. They must begin looking at these problems now. It is with this thought in mind that the Los Angeles Public Library offers this booklist. The library shelves contain no easy solutions or pat answers, but they can provide some of the background needed to understand the events of the past and the discussions of the future.

The Los Angeles Public Library is not endorsing any particular viewpoint other than that it is necessary to read about and understand the problems at hand. None of these books will answer all the whys of the August riots but they are a beginning in the search for answers. There may be, hopefully, a heavy run on the books listed here and so we would ask library visitors to talk to their local librarians about other materials on these subjects. Only through a better informed citizenry can we hope to meet any of the major social, cultural and economic problems that we face.

FROM SLAVERY TO FREEDOM

THE NEGRO VANGUARD Richard Bardolph Studies of Negro leaders from 1770 to 1959.	326.973 B247
BEFORE THE MAYFLOWER Lerone Bennett The history of the Negro in America.	326.973 B471
100 YEARS OF NEGRO FREEDOM Arna W. Bontemps Based upon portraits of leaders from Frederick Douglass to Martin Luther King.	326.973 B722-1
13 AGAINST THE ODDS Edwin R. Embree Brief portraits of famous Negro-Americans.	326.973 E53-3

One way librarians attempted to address racial unrest during this period was by generating booklists of works by Black authors, circa 1965
Institutional Collection, Special Collections

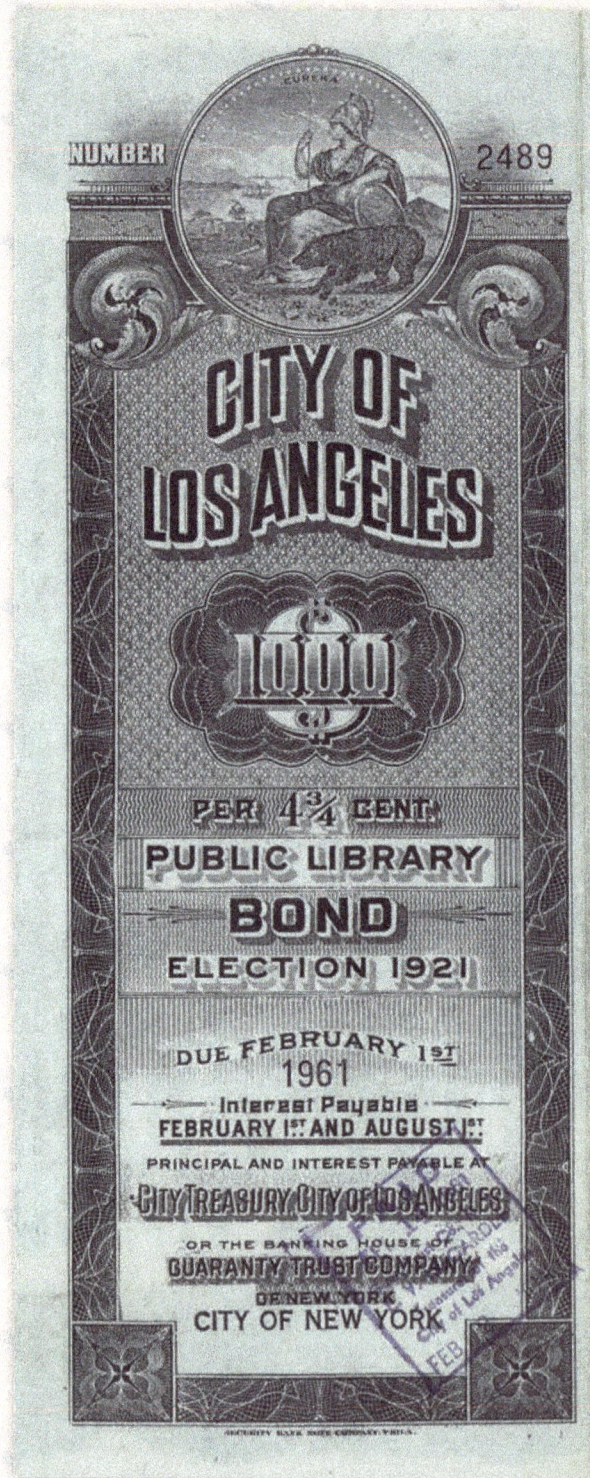

City of Los Angeles,
Public Library Bond, 1921
Institutional Archive,
Special Collections

Bonds! Bonds! Bonds!

Community Support for the Library has been most evident in the support of bonds, propositions and measures which have helped build the Central Library and nearly all of the branches that exist today. Not all of the bonds passed, but most did, and to this day the Library has remained sustainable thanks to the support of Angelenos.

CITY OF LOS ANGELES

1000   **1000**

PUBLIC LIBRARY BOND
ELECTION 1921

NO. **2489**   NO. **2489**

City of Los Angeles, Public Library Bond, 1921
Institutional Archive, Special Collections

Proposition C informational
pamphlet, 1957
Institutional Archive,
Special Collections

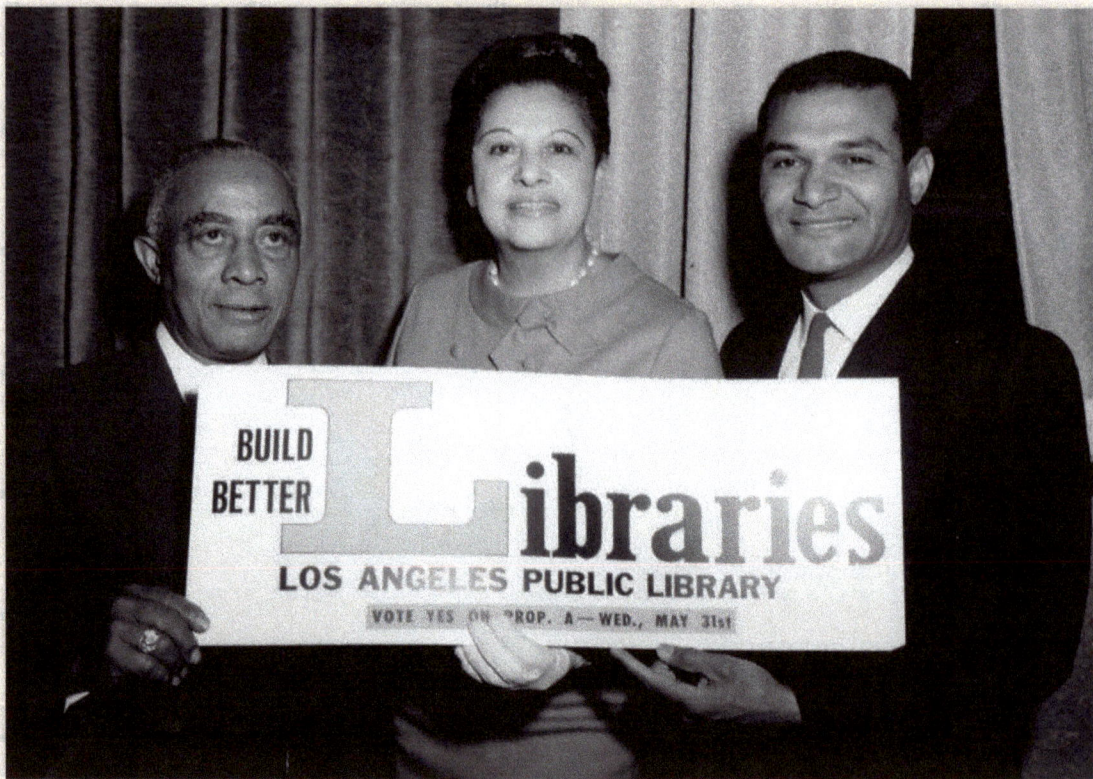

Councilmembers Gilbert Lindsay (left) and Billy Mills, endorse Proposition A with Library Commissioner Leontyne King, 1967
Institutional Collection

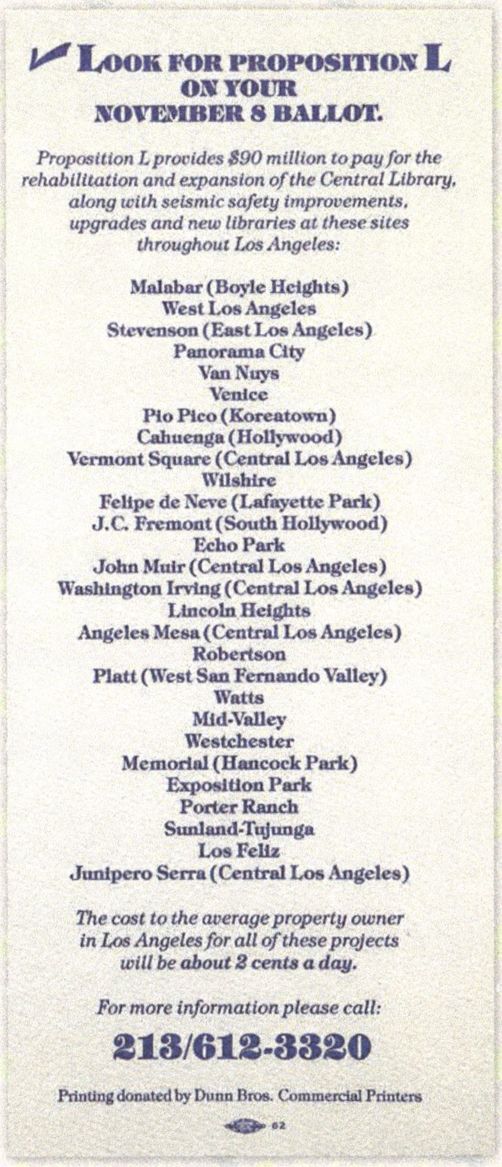

✔ LOOK FOR PROPOSITION L ON YOUR NOVEMBER 8 BALLOT.

Proposition L provides $90 million to pay for the rehabilitation and expansion of the Central Library, along with seismic safety improvements, upgrades and new libraries at these sites throughout Los Angeles:

Malabar (Boyle Heights)
West Los Angeles
Stevenson (East Los Angeles)
Panorama City
Van Nuys
Venice
Pio Pico (Koreatown)
Cahuenga (Hollywood)
Vermont Square (Central Los Angeles)
Wilshire
Felipe de Neve (Lafayette Park)
J.C. Fremont (South Hollywood)
Echo Park
John Muir (Central Los Angeles)
Washington Irving (Central Los Angeles)
Lincoln Heights
Angeles Mesa (Central Los Angeles)
Robertson
Platt (West San Fernando Valley)
Watts
Mid-Valley
Westchester
Memorial (Hancock Park)
Exposition Park
Porter Ranch
Sunland-Tujunga
Los Feliz
Junipero Serra (Central Los Angeles)

The cost to the average property owner in Los Angeles for all of these projects will be about 2 cents a day.

For more information please call:

213/612-3320

Printing donated by Dunn Bros. Commercial Printers

Proposition L informational pamphlet, 1988
Institutional Archive, Special Collections

THE BOARD OF LIBRARY COMMISSIONERS
LA JUNTA DE COMISIONADOS DE LA BIBLIOTECA

invites you to the / *le invita a Ud. a*

GRAND OPENING CEREMONY
LA CEREMONIA DE APERTURA

of the new / *de la nueva*

EL SERENO BRANCH
Los Angeles Public Library
5226 Huntington Drive, So.

Friday, September 17, 2004
viernes, 17 de septiembre de 2004
10 a.m.

James K. Hahn   **Antonio R. Villaraigosa**
Mayor   Councilmember
City of Los Angeles   District 14

ADA accommodation available upon request.
Se acomodan incapacitados a petición.

Grand opening invitation for a branch made possible
by the 1998 Proposition DD
Institutional Archive

Save
L.A. Public Library
www.savethelibrary.org

Measure L sticker, 2011
Courtesy of Christina Rice

Steps Forward, Steps Back

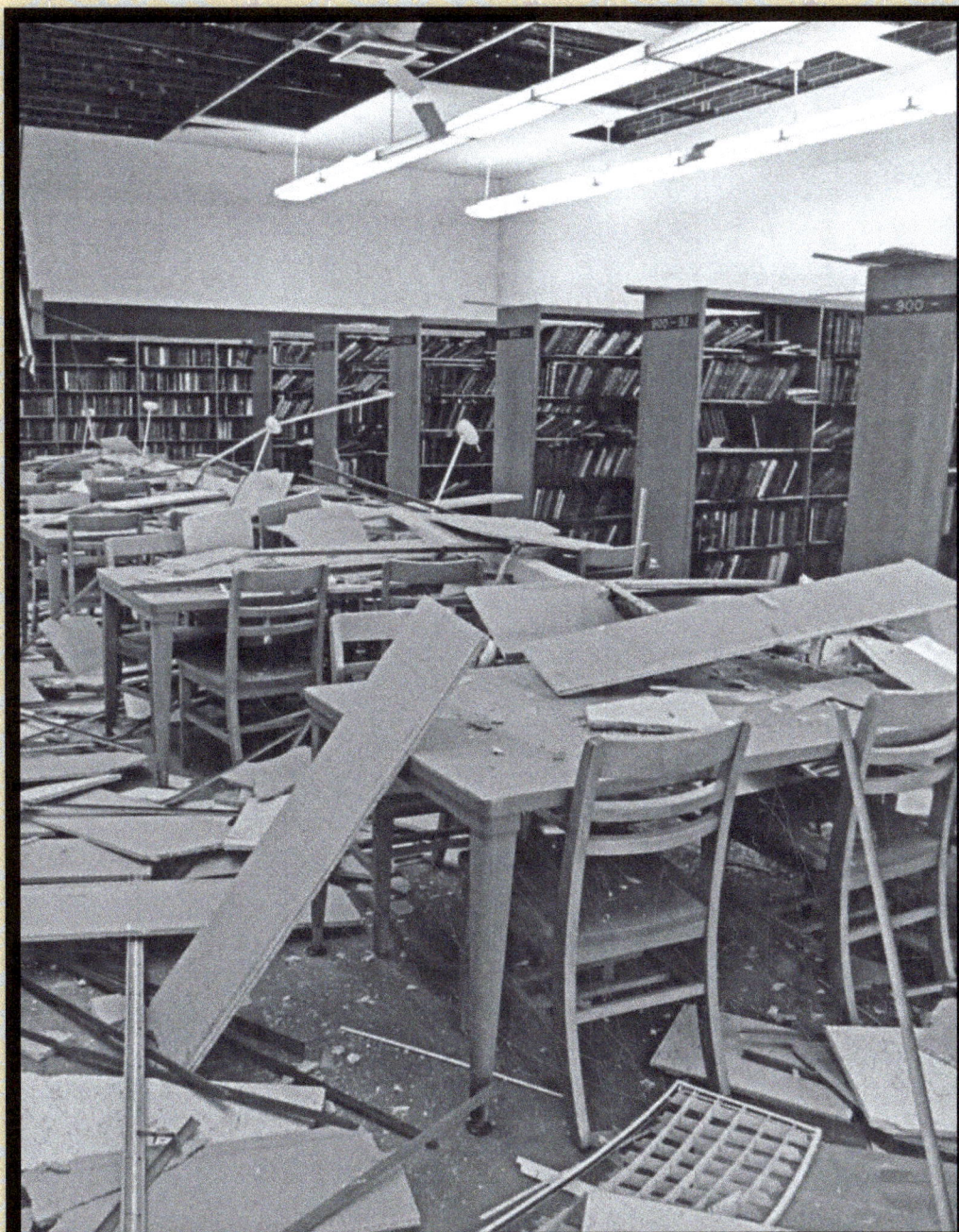

Earthquake damage at the Granada Hills Branch Library, 1971
Institutional Collection

In the early 1970s, the Sylmar earthquake permanently closed older and beloved branches in the inner city, and public service for these neighborhoods had to be relocated to temporary quarters, with the prospect of replacement facilities uncertain. Subsequent earthquakes with epicenters in Whittier (1987) and Northridge (1994) would cause temporary closures of branches, but would have far less of an impact than the Sylmar earthquake.

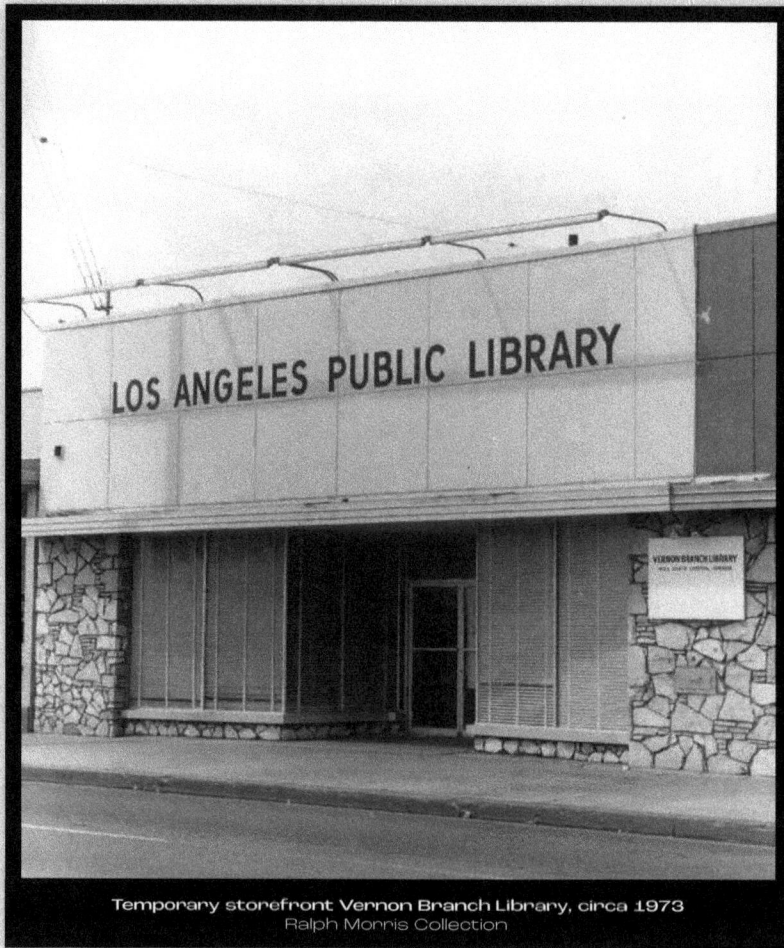

Temporary storefront Vernon Branch Library, circa 1973
Ralph Morris Collection

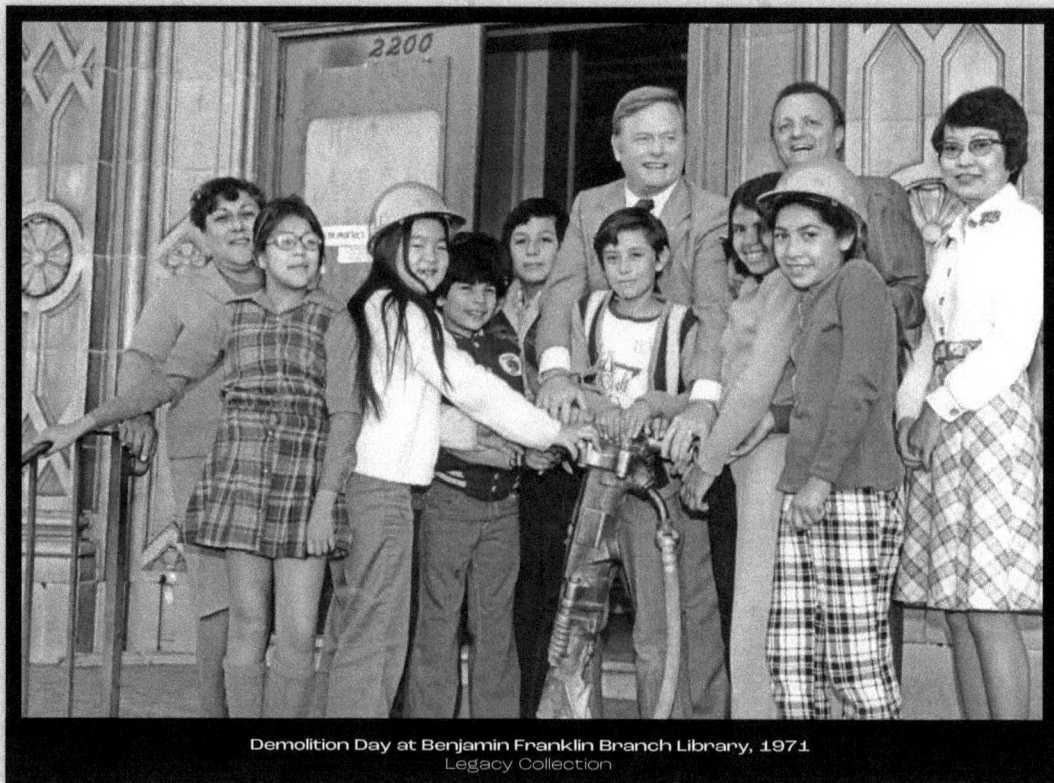

Demolition Day at Benjamin Franklin Branch Library, 1971
Legacy Collection

REPORT ON LEGALITY OF BRANCH

LIBRARY FUNDING DISPARITIES

BURT PINES, City Attorney of Los Angeles
by JOHN E. McDERMOTT, Deputy City Attorney
1800 City Hall East
Los Angeles, California 90012
(213) 485-6398

Report on Legality of Branch Library Funding Disparities,
Office of the City Attorney of Los Angeles, 1975

SUMMARY OF DISCUSSION:

      Based on information available to our office,
disparities in expenditures and other resources among
the City's 61 branch and regional community libraries
are substantial, and appear to impact adversely on
minority communities. Nearly twice as much money is
allocated to libraries serving predominantly white
communities as to libraries serving predominantly
minority communities. Indeed, with respect to every
relevant library resource for which data is available
to us, that data indicates that libraries serving
minority communities receive substantially fewer resources than libraries serving predominantly white
communities. These resources include money, staff,
library materials, hours of service, and age, size
and value of facilities. These disparities in library
resources raise serious questions under applicable fed-
eral and state constitutional and statutory law,
including the following: (1) the equal protection pro-
visions of the United States Constitution, (2) the

Library access in the inner city lagged behind the suburbs where so many new branches had recently opened. A report outlined the lack of funding equity and showed how the City was spending less on minority communities in older neighborhoods. Central Library badly needed renovation, and some discussion advocated redirecting those funds to renovate the older branches and strengthen outreach to underserved communities.

Dedication of the Hollywood Branch Library, designed by Frank Gehry, 1986
Herald Examiner Collection

While there had been small arson fires at several branches throughout the sixties and seventies, nothing prepared the Library for the 1982 conflagration at the Hollywood Branch Library, one of the Library's most popular and storied locations. The fire devastated the collection and building, but the response from the community was as strong as it was immediate. Celebrities offered their support, whether money (Johnny Carson) or services (Orson Welles), and the overall community support led to a new Library Branch designed by a star architect. This successful effort would provide a ready template for the recovery of Central Library after its fire just a few years later.

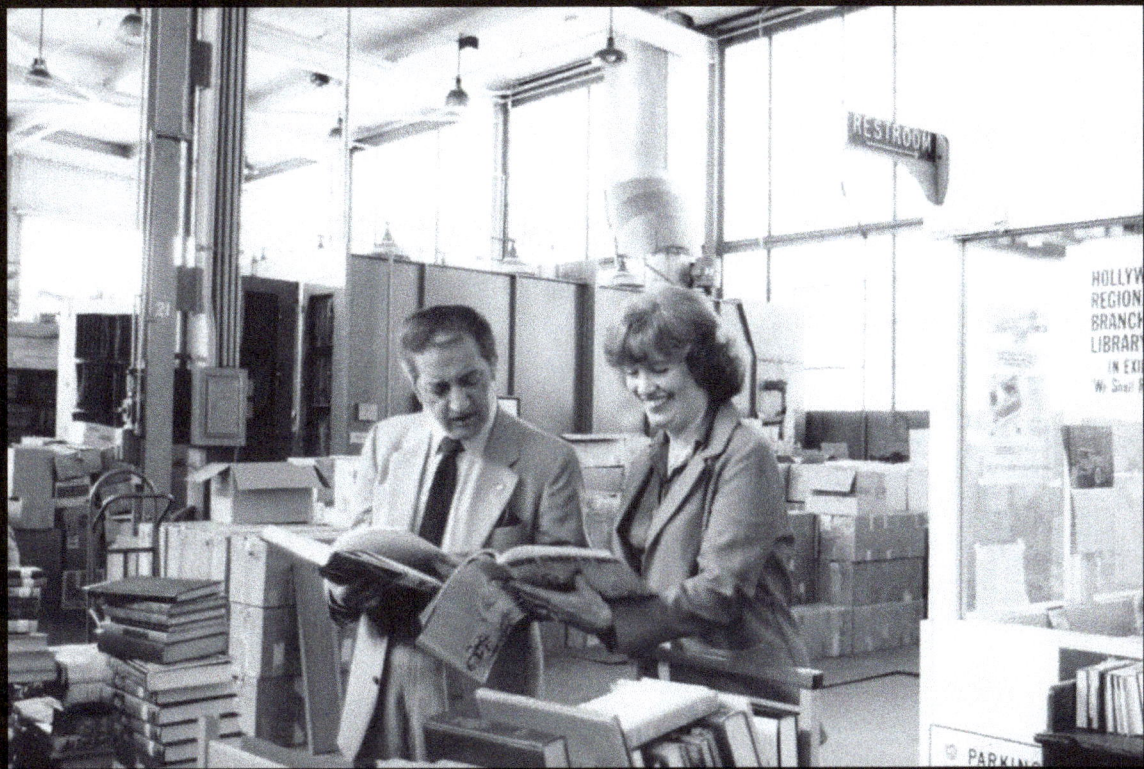

Staff member Georgette Todd gives actor Danny Thomas a tour of a book drying facility
following the Hollywood Branch fire, 1982
Institutional Collection

Hollywood Branch Library fire aftermath, 1982
Institutional Collection

Chinatown Branch Library, 1977
Institutional Collection

Chinatown Branch Library opening day, 1977
Institutional Collection

In Chinatown, neighborhood associations lobbied for a new branch that had a strong focus on Chinese language materials. Initially the Los Angeles Public Library considered that Central Library could fulfill the needs of this nearby neighborhood, but eventually responded to the community outcry for more focused representation, and Chinatown received its own branch in 1977. Members of the Little Tokyo community enjoyed similar success during this period, transitioning from a regular bookmobile stop to an experimental branch, then to a permanent branch library.

Howard Jarvis and Paul Gann, Proposition 13's most visible advocates, celebrate its passage, 1978
Ken Papaleo, Herald Examiner Collection

The passage of Proposition 13 in 1978 slashed property taxes and resulted in massive cuts to government services. For a library system that, as created by the City Charter, had a budget heavily based on property tax assessments, Prop 13 was a blow as powerful as an earthquake.

Temporary library card, 1935
Institutional Archive, Special Collections

Patron checkout log, 1946
Institutional Archive, Special Collections

Library card, 1960
Institutional Archive, Special Collections

Check it Out !

A wonderful rite of passage occurs when a person obtains their first library card, followed by checking out their first book. In the age of automation, paper cards were replaced with barcoded plastic cards. Yet even with the rise of digital recordkeeping, the physical library card is as compelling as ever, as is evident by the popularity of limited edition library cards.

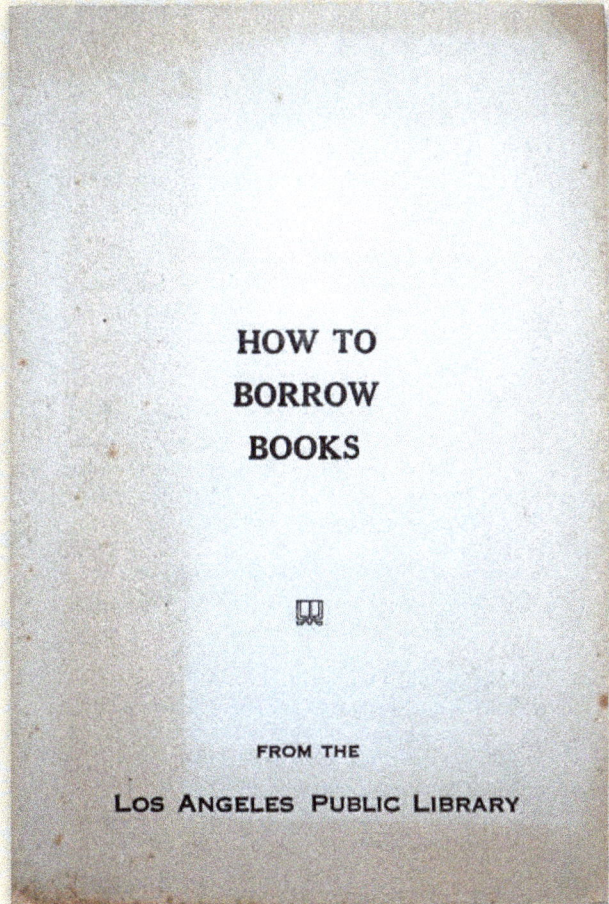

Patron checkout log, 1909
Institutional Archive, Special Collections

HOW TO
BORROW
BOOKS

FROM THE

LOS ANGELES PUBLIC LIBRARY

How to Borrow Books From the Los Angeles Public Library
Institutional Archive, Special Collections

Punch cards used for tracking circulation on individual books, 1970s-1980s
Courtesy of Pearl Yonezawa

LOS ANGELES
PUBLIC LIBRARY

57291429 00   EXP. 11-20-96

KAMAL F AZEEZ
5826 VIRGINIA AV #1
LOS ANGELES   CALIF 90038

Final paper library card before automation, used circa 1971-1993
Courtesy of Pearl Yonezawa

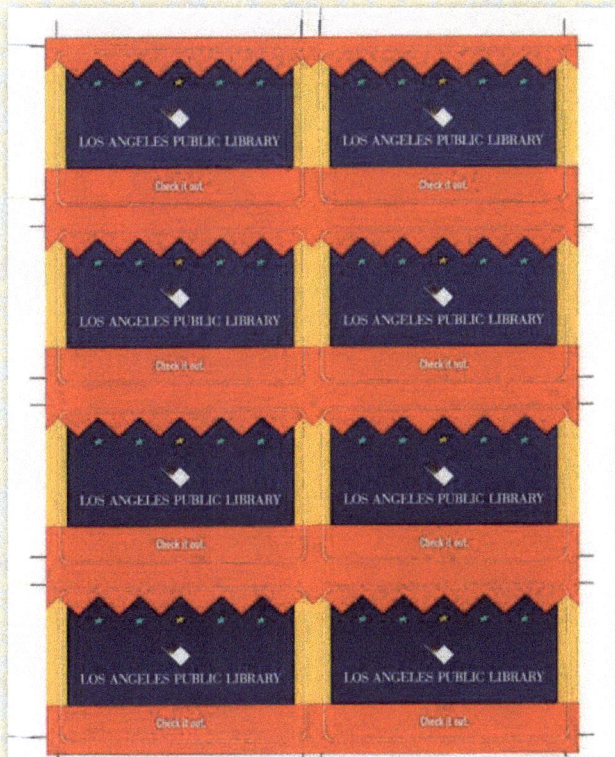

Sheets of plastic library cards issued after switch to automated circulation system, 1993
Institutional Archive, Special Collections

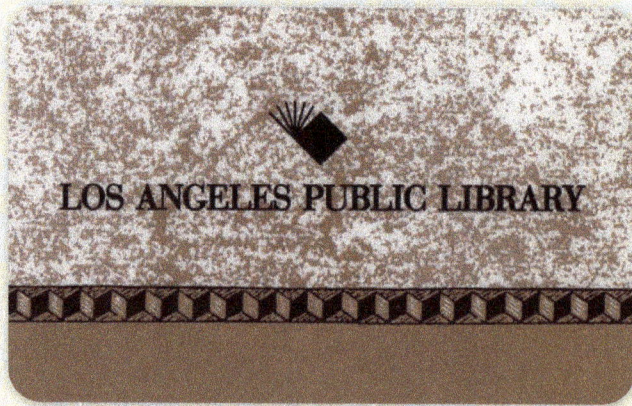

Commemorative library card issued to attendees
of a gala reception sponsored by the
Library Foundation of Los Angeles, 1993
Institutional Archive, Special Collections

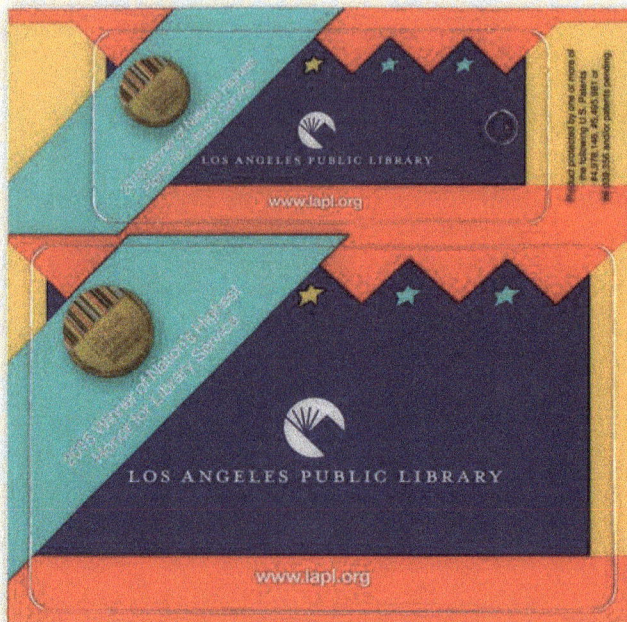

Commemorative library card, 2015
Institutional Archive, Special Collections

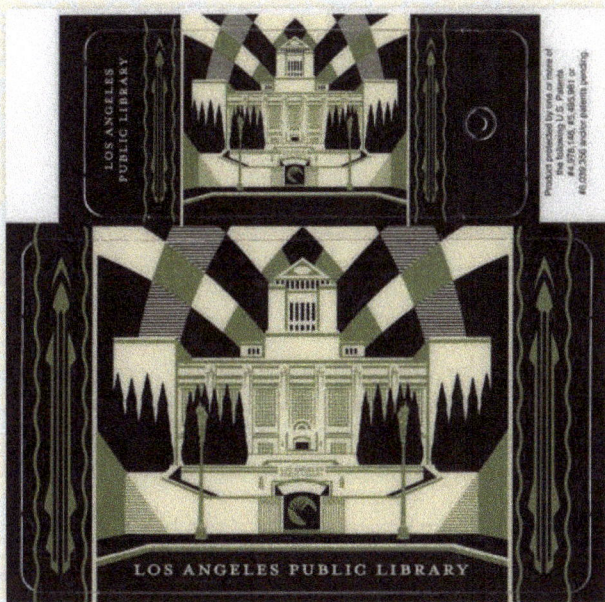

Limited edition artist library card by Shepard Fairey, 2016
Institutional Archive, Special Collections

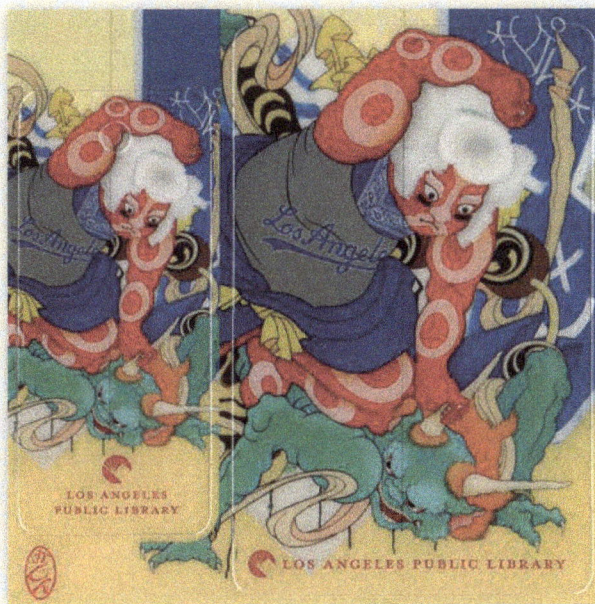

Limited edition artist library card by Gajin Fujita, 2019
Institutional Archive, Special Collections

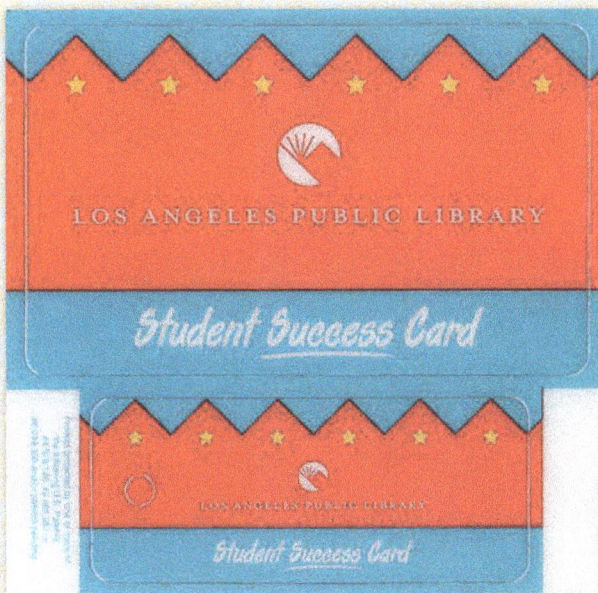

Student Success library card, 2016
Institutional Archive, Special Collections

Teacher library card, 2017
Institutional Archive, Special Collections

Changes, Challenges, and Conviction

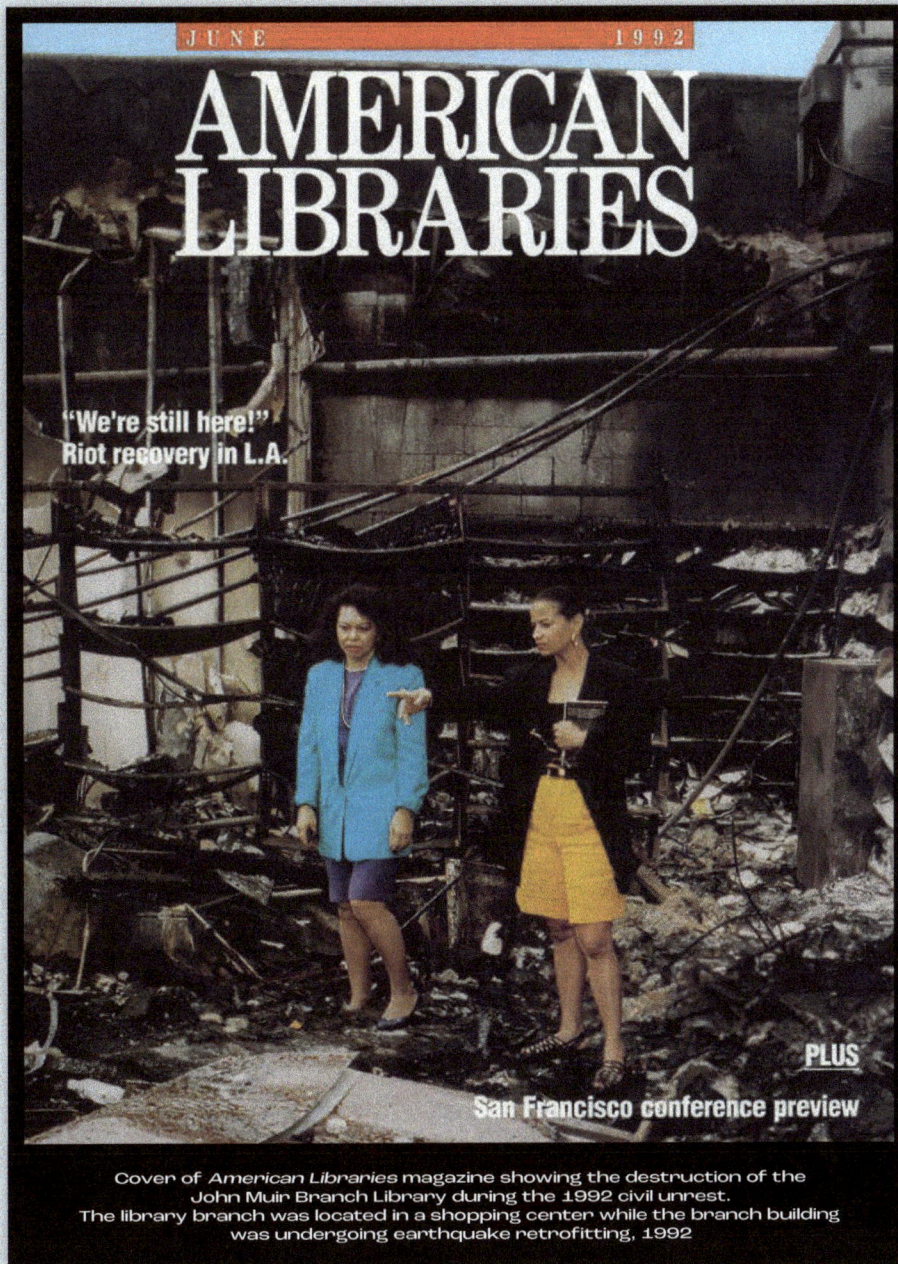

Cover of *American Libraries* magazine showing the destruction of the John Muir Branch Library during the 1992 civil unrest. The library branch was located in a shopping center while the branch building was undergoing earthquake retrofitting, 1992

In 1989, Proposition One was passed for more funding to strengthen the branch library system, just a few years prior to the destruction caused by civil unrest following the Rodney King verdict in 1992 and the Northridge earthquake in 1994. Even though things looked bleak, the funding provided by the successful proposition set the stage for the next big period of growth. Prop One built three new libraries and enabled 24 existing branches to be rebuilt, renovated or expanded, and use of city branch libraries exploded.

Exposition Park Branch Library Rendering, Tetra Design, 2000
Courtesy Los Angeles Public Library

"LAPL for the Nineties" was a system-wide plan that incorporated community needs in a dedicated strategy of inclusion in providing service to the many diverse cultures of Los Angeles. Focused on making a positive difference in the daily lives of inhabitants, the plan would guide library programming and branch building during the renovations and expansion of the next decade. The success of Proposition One led to the passage of Proposition DD in 1998. It led to the improvement, construction and rehabilitation of 32 branches, including 14 completely new branches, five of which were located in areas of the City that had never enjoyed library services.

Little Tokyo Branch Library Rendering, A.J. Lumsden & Associates, Charles Walton Associates, circa 2000
Courtesy Los Angeles Public Library

Playa Vista Branch Library Rendering, Johnson Fain Partners, circa 2000
Courtesy Los Angeles Public Library

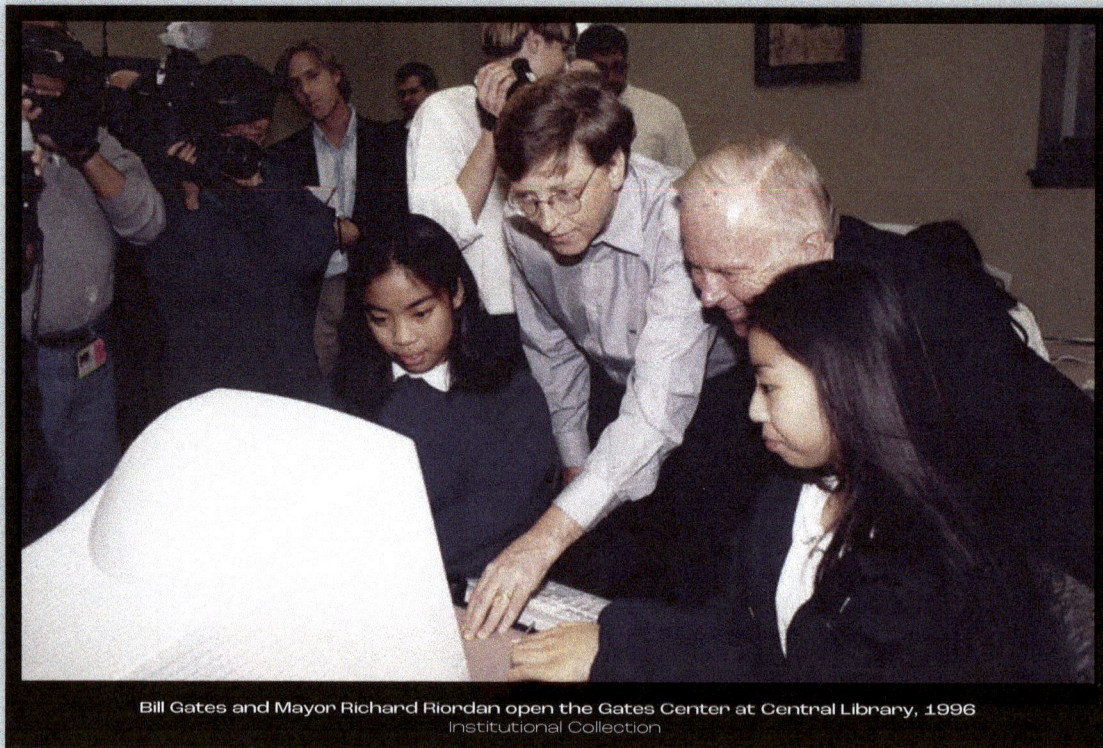
Bill Gates and Mayor Richard Riordan open the Gates Center at Central Library, 1996
Institutional Collection

Dial-In Access
To The
Catalog
Of The

LOS ANGELES
PUBLIC LIBRARY

(213) 623-6455

The original information highway

LOS ANGELES
PUBLIC LIBRARY

125th year Anniversary

"Original Information Highway," 1996
Institutional Collection

The Los Angeles Public Library has long been a pioneer in technology. Among other innovations, the Library was the first in the nation to employ a computerized record-keeping system (1971), and was also the first public library anywhere with a public-access networked computer terminal (1973). It was also one of the earliest public libraries to start digitizing its unique special collections. Therefore it was no surprise that, in the 1990s, the Los Angeles Public Library was one of the earliest adopters of digital technologies, and was a large proponent of ensuring that residents without service to the newest information modes would not be left behind on the "information superhighway." Thanks to innovative public-private partnerships, the Library was able to make real its commitment to bridging the digital divide and ensuring technology equity.

Staff encourage support for Measure L at the Sunset & Vermont Metro Station, 2011
Courtesy of the Librarians Guild

Budget woes caused by the 2008 financial crisis resulted in layoffs and the first change in the City Charter in more than a hundred years. In response, Library staff and administration supported Measure L, which amended the Charter and provided the basis for more flexible funding that laid the groundwork for a more stable future for the Library's programs and services.

Patrons utilize the "Library to Go" service at the Los Feliz Branch Library, 2020
Courtesy of the Los Angeles Public Library

One of the most difficult challenges in the history of the Los Angeles Public Library was the COVID-19 pandemic, which caused the first system-wide shutdown in the Library's history of service. As with so many institutions, the Library's public services were disrupted. However, the disruption was brief because the Library proved adaptable once again. Library at Home, Library to Go and Internet Hot Spots provided access to the Library's physical and electronic resources, and the Library's makerspace, Octavia Lab, repurposed itself to create more than 126,000 face shields for local hospitals.

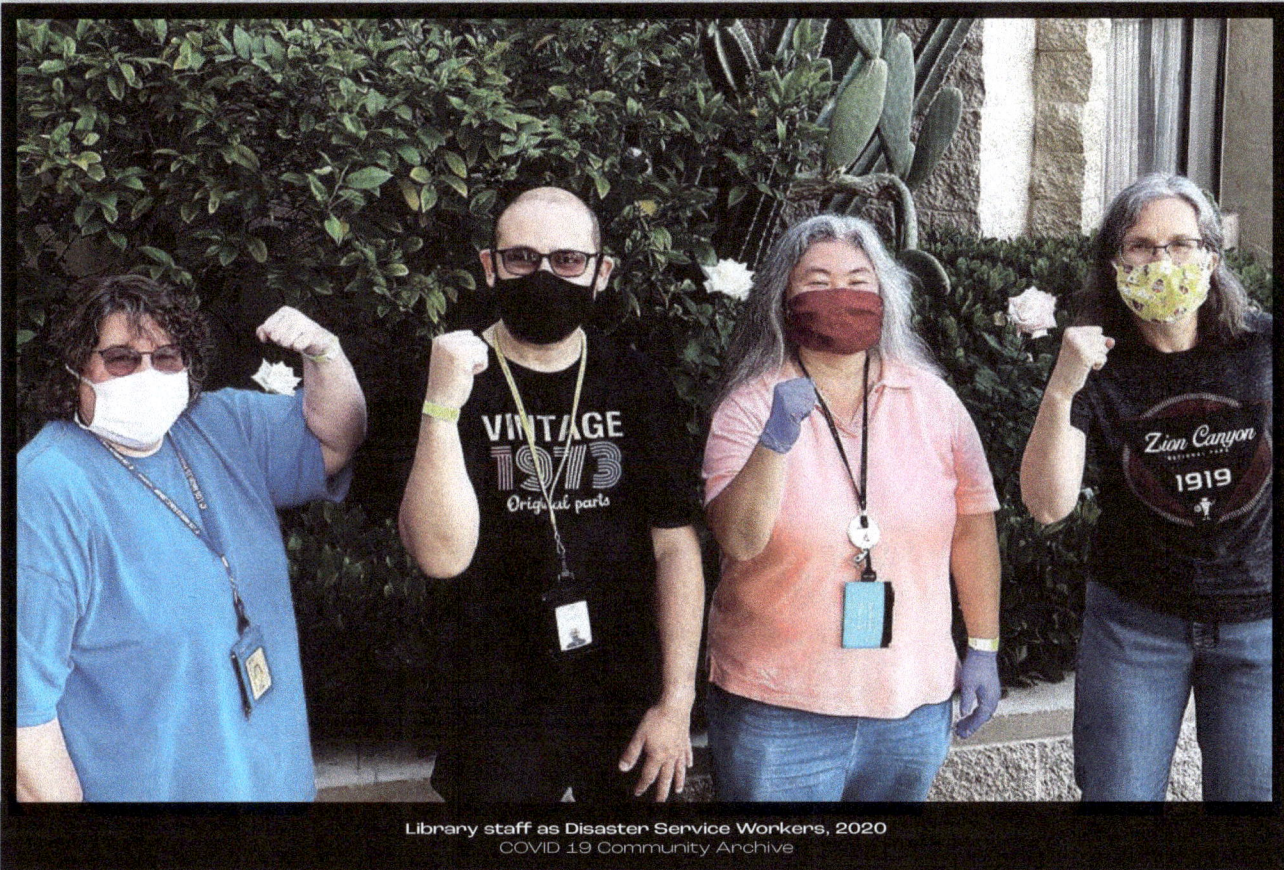

Library staff as Disaster Service Workers, 2020
COVID 19 Community Archive

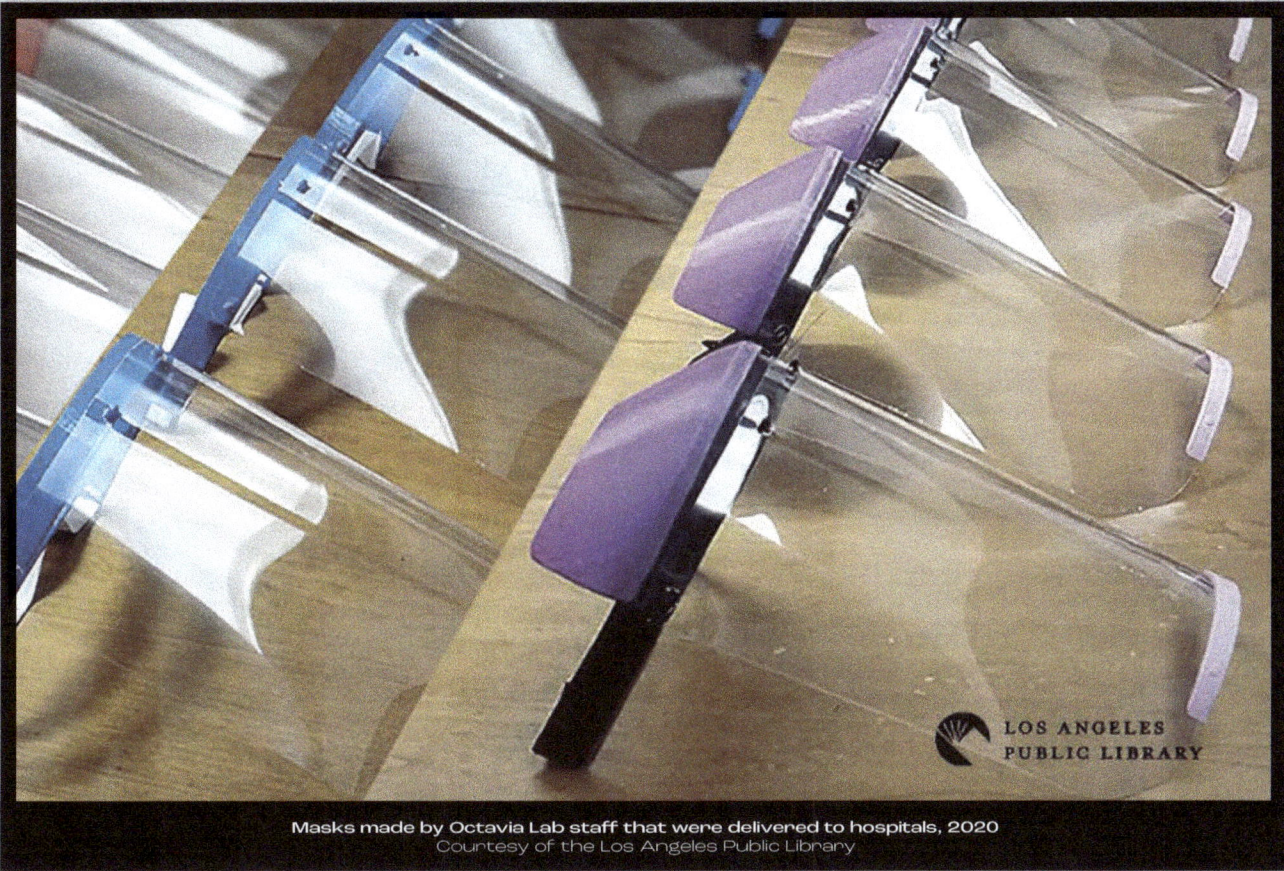

LOS ANGELES
PUBLIC LIBRARY

Masks made by Octavia Lab staff that were delivered to hospitals, 2020
Courtesy of the Los Angeles Public Library

Bookplate, used from approximately 1903-1925
Institutional Archive, Special Collections

Bookplate, designed by Crocker Litho,
used from 1889-1903
Institutional Archive, Special Collections

Bookplates

The Library has used bookplates for nearly its entire history. After the Board of Governors was established in 1889, one of their first acts was to create a bookplate through a design contest. The "Angel" plate was printed in two colors of ink—green and terracotta—for circulating and reference books respectively. It was replaced by the circular image containing a book with light rays emanating from it and a Latin quote that more or less means "the glory of the light of the city." With the opening of Central Library, a new design featuring a central triangle was introduced, which was used either as a regular collection bookplate or to indicate a special collection or a bequest. After the fire, the commemorative bookplates were again used to thank donors for their support of the Library in the Save the Books program.

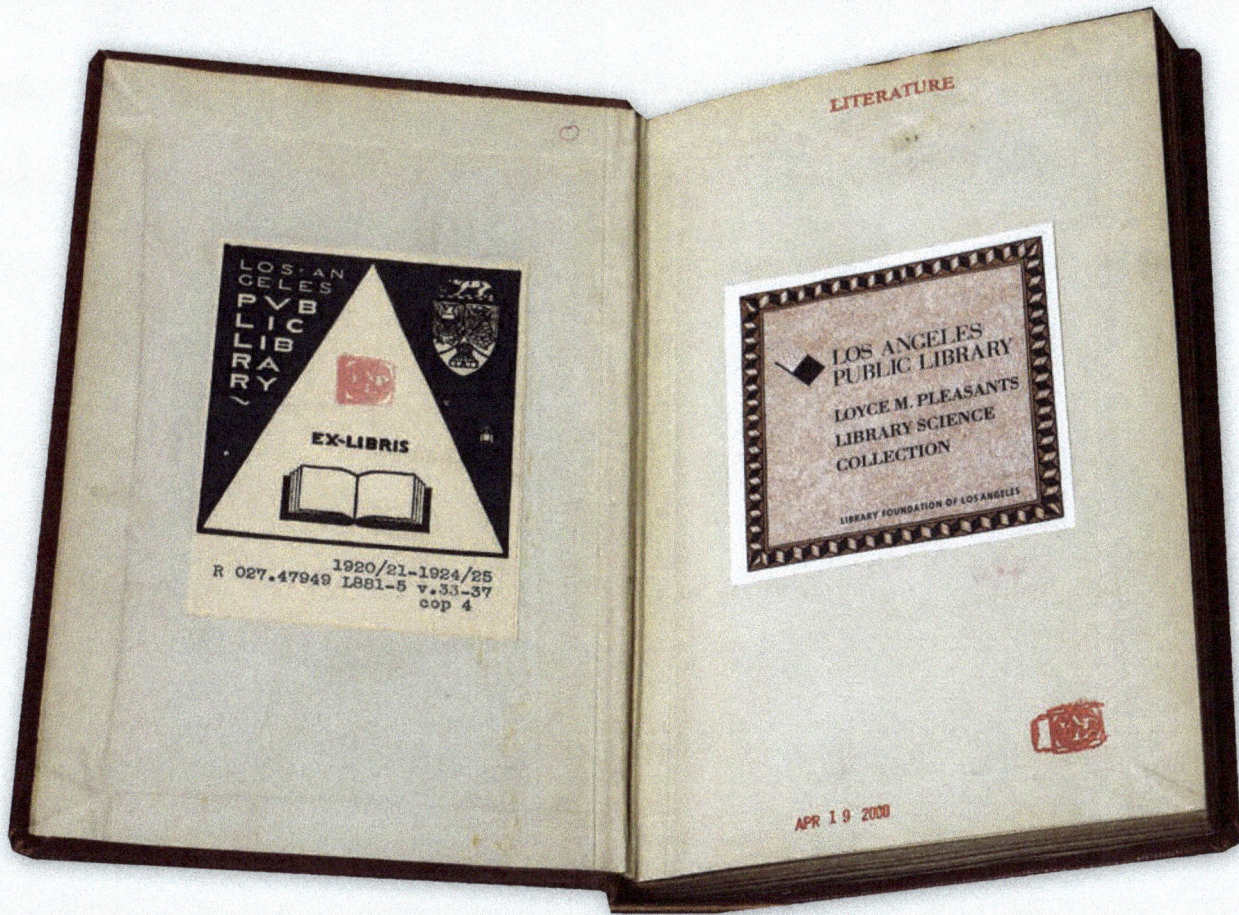

Save the Books named collection bookplate (right), undated
Literature & Fiction Department

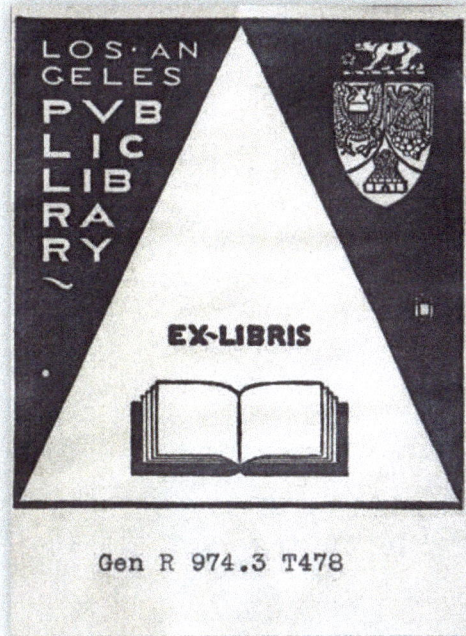

Triangle bookplate, circa 1934
Institutional Archive,
Special Collections

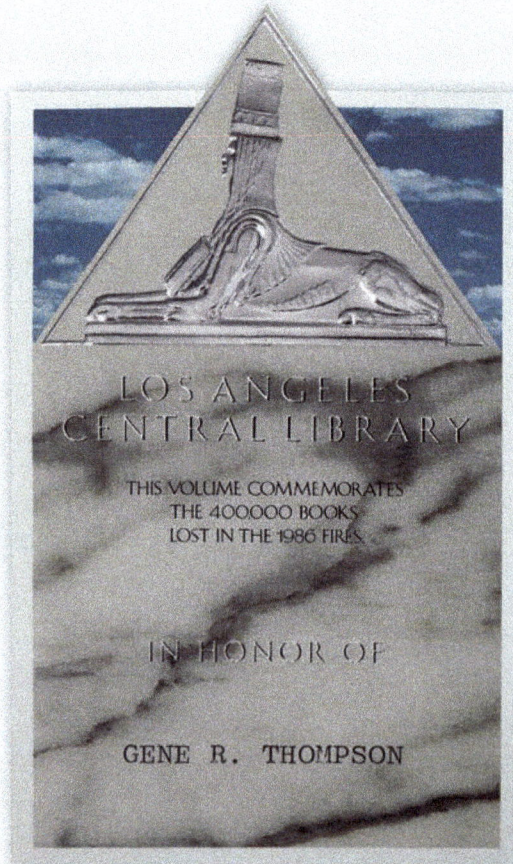

Save the Books memorial bookplate, circa 1990
Literature & Fiction Department

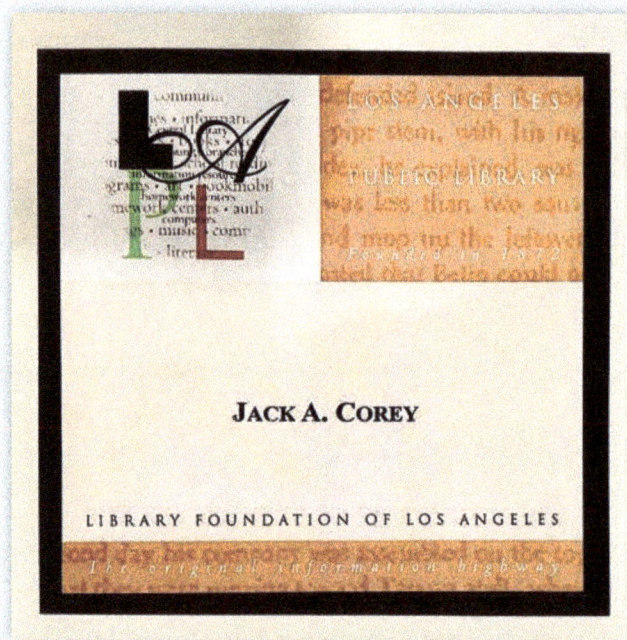

125th anniversary bookplate, 1997
Literature & Fiction Department

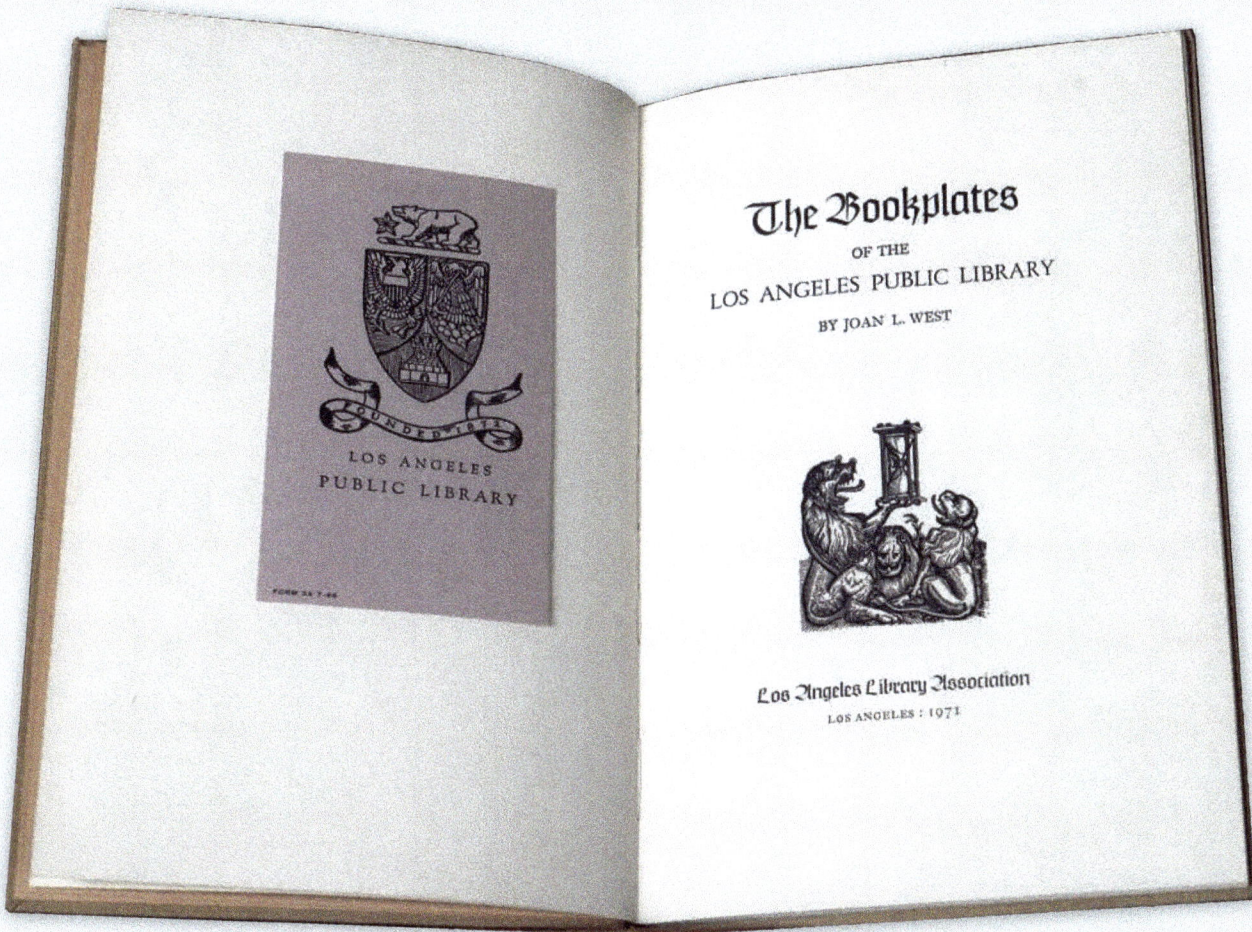

Bookplate featuring the City seal, undated
Bookplates of the Los Angeles Public Library by Joan L. West, 1971
Literature & Fiction Department

Central Library

Newspaper editorial graphic, 1921
Los Angeles Record

During the first fifty years of the Los Angeles Public Library, the City grew by nearly 10,000 percent. Throughout the 1910s, the Library and its boosters proposed a bond for a permanent central building, arguing that Los Angeles was the only city of its size without an established main library and no plans to build one. The implication was that the City would remain second rate until a dedicated central location was erected. When the 1920 census reflected that, for the first time, L.A.'s population had surged past San Francisco to become the largest city in the state, Library supporters shamelessly appealed to the pride of Angelenos in order to get a bond passed that would build the Central Library. Proponents also used modern communication technology—in the week before the election, a short film donated by the motion picture industry in support of the bond issue was screened in the ten largest L.A. theaters, and in lesser theaters, slides were projected before every performance, promoting a suitable building for the Los Angeles Public Library.

State Normal School, 1918
Security Pacific National Bank Collection

The 1921 bond Issue passed and made $2.5 million available for building a permanent library as well as branches. In 1922 the City Council deeded Normal Hill to the Library but with strings attached. The most onerous required the Library to pay the cost of demolishing the existing enormous building that had previously housed the State Normal School. After contentious wrangling with the City Council, the Library Board paid, paving the way for a permanent structure.

Central Library under construction, 1926
W.A. Hughes, Institutional Collection

The Central Library was the final effort of architect Bertram Grosvenor Goodhue, who intended that the architecture would integrate art, which had often been considered ornamental, into the design. For instance, the sculptures by Lee Lawrie would symbolize learning and culture, and thus stress that function of the building. In addition, the building is meant to be read "like a book," in the words of Goodhue's partner, iconographer Hartley Burr Alexander, who chose the theme "Light of Learning" as well as the images and texts adorning Central Library which express that theme. Sadly, Goodhue passed away during the construction, and never saw the realization of his last design.

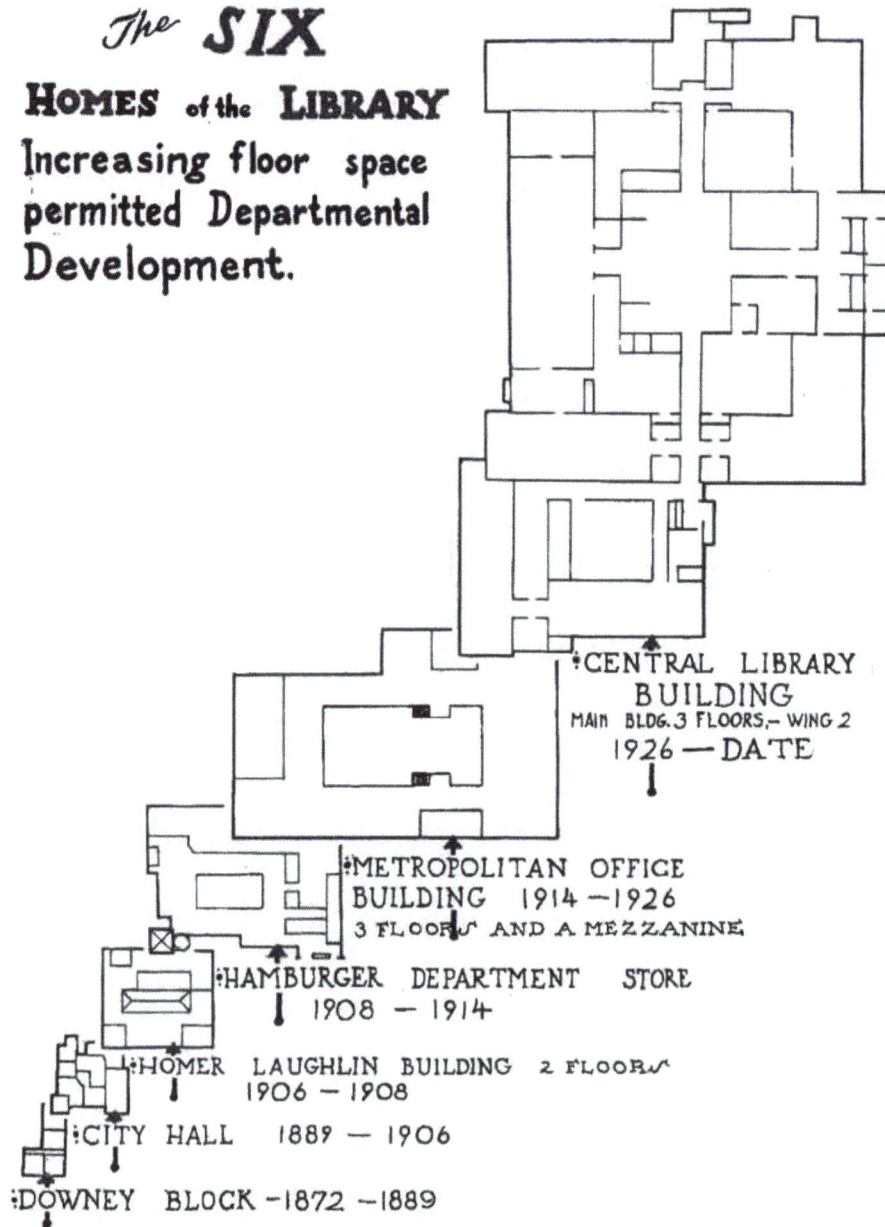

The SIX
HOMES of the LIBRARY
Increasing floor space permitted Departmental Development.

CENTRAL LIBRARY BUILDING
MAIN BLDG. 3 FLOORS,- WING 2
1926 — DATE

METROPOLITAN OFFICE BUILDING 1914 —1926
3 FLOORS AND A MEZZANINE

HAMBURGER DEPARTMENT STORE 1908 — 1914

HOMER LAUGHLIN BUILDING 2 FLOORS 1906 — 1908

CITY HALL 1889 — 1906

DOWNEY BLOCK —1872 —1889

Floorplans of all Central Libraries, *Forty-eighth Annual Report of the Board of Library Commissioners of the Los Angeles Public Library* for the year ending June 30, 1936

The story of the Los Angeles Public Library's main library building prior to the current building is the story of never having enough room. The growth of the city was so rapid during the first fifty years of the Central Library that, as soon as new quarters were found and celebrated, they were outgrown and a new search for temporary quarters would start, as debate raged about where and how a permanent location would be built.

View of completed Central Library, including Eastlawn, and the Richfield Building and the California Club under construction, circa 1929
Institutional Collection

Central Library debuted in downtown Los Angeles to many accolades. At its opening, it was declared "one of the noblest buildings in America," and other commentators gushed that the building was a "tremendous step forward in local architecture that imitated no style or school" and represented a movement from "colonial Spanish influence into the metropolis of the future." Much later, Ray Bradbury paid tribute to its style, saying that Central Library looked like "Tomorrow itself" and that, other than the Music Center, it was the "only building downtown worth looking at."

Rotunda prior to murals, 1926
Mott Studios, Institutional Collection

Workmen stand on different levels of a scaffold as they work on the west wall of Dean Cornwell's murals; Dean Cornwell can be seen wearing a dark suit and standing on the left (bottom) of the ladder, 1932
Institutional Collection

The Rotunda was the core of the building, and its murals were created by famed illustrator Dean Cornwell. Like Renaissance tapestries, each mural panel tells a romanticized, if sometimes inaccurate and questionable, story of an era in California history. Eight smaller panels below offer two sets of allegories: the conquering of the elements, and the arts of civilization.

THE·WORLD·IS·MY·BOOK

The Children's entrance at Central Library
Institutional Collection

The Central Library was designed with a special welcome for its youngest patrons: a separate entrance for them that led to the Children's Literature Department and opened out into the great East Lawn. This portal was eliminated when the modern Tom Bradley Wing was built in 1993, but the door was preserved and relocated to the entrance of the current Taper Auditorium.

Genealogy Department (demolished), circa 1930
Institutional Collection

Music Room (demolished), circa 1926
Mott Studios, Institutional Collection

Foreign Department (now Meeting Room B), circa 1930
Mott Studios, Institutional Collection

Literature Department (now the Children's Literature workroom), circa 1930
Institutional Collection

Long before a permanent building became a reality, the core library collection was organized into subject departments with specialists overseeing each area. This approach evolved into a central reference library. These in-depth reference collections were developed with current topical titles, and the librarians working with these collections continually honed their expertise for the benefit of the general public as well as the business, legal and academic communities. The development of these Subject Departments was essential in determining the design of Central Library. The floor plan was specifically adapted to ten specialized subjects, each with their own reading rooms, stacks, and staff rooms.

History Department (now Children's Literature), circa 1965
Marv Newton, Institutional Collection

Science Department (now the Getty Gallery), circa 1930
Mott Studios, Institutional Collection

Art Department (now the Sports Room), circa 1965
Marv Newton, Institutional Collection

Business Department (now the Cafe), circa 1965
Marv Newton, Institutional Collection

Fiction Department (now Teen'Scape), 1981
William Reagh, Los Angeles Photographers Collection

Social Science Department (now the Children's Literature Picture Book Room), circa 1965
Institutional Collection

Overcrowded Science Department, circa 1970
Institutional Collection

Central Library's success produced its own problems, becoming such an essential part of daily Los Angeles life that its footprint was almost instantly too small for a city that was growing by leaps and bounds. The postwar boom resulted in Los Angeles becoming the third largest metropolis in America, and the G.I. Bill ensured that a steady stream of students constantly flocked to Central Library. The building became overcrowded.

Central Library gardens are demolished to make way for a staff parking lot, 1969
Herald Examiner Collection

This overcrowding, along with the future-forward, mid-Century focus on downtown "renewal," meant that by the 1960s, the building was on the road to demolition. In 1967, after a bond issue for a new Central Library failed, some City Council members believed the city would never get a new central building through bond measures. A new building would therefore have to be privately financed, with one Council Member also suggesting that "branches stand a better chance by themselves because people hesitate to travel downtown." Many believed if a new Central Library were to be built, it should be a completely new and modern structure. In 1969, the same year that Central Library was placed on the National Register of Historic Places, the Board of Library Commissioners approved paving over Flower Street gardens for a parking lot.

Cramped working conditions, circa 1970s
Institutional Collection

Given the cramped and dangerous working conditions of a Central Library built for a much smaller city, both the staff and administration wanted a new modern library. During the Library's centennial year, Central Library staff even signed a petition protesting unsafe working conditions, and the Los Angeles Fire Department cited Central Library for 26 fire and safety violations.

Charles Luckman's design, c1979
Herald Examiner Collection

Despite its many detractors, the old Central Library structure did have allies in architectural preservationists, but the stronger argument against building a completely new modern library was shrinking budgets. Large scale schemes were scrapped and plans were made to build a remodeled and modernized Central Library structure that would have included escalators in the Rotunda. For the Los Angeles Public Library, the only reason to be thankful for Prop 13 was that it took away funding for that misguided renovation!

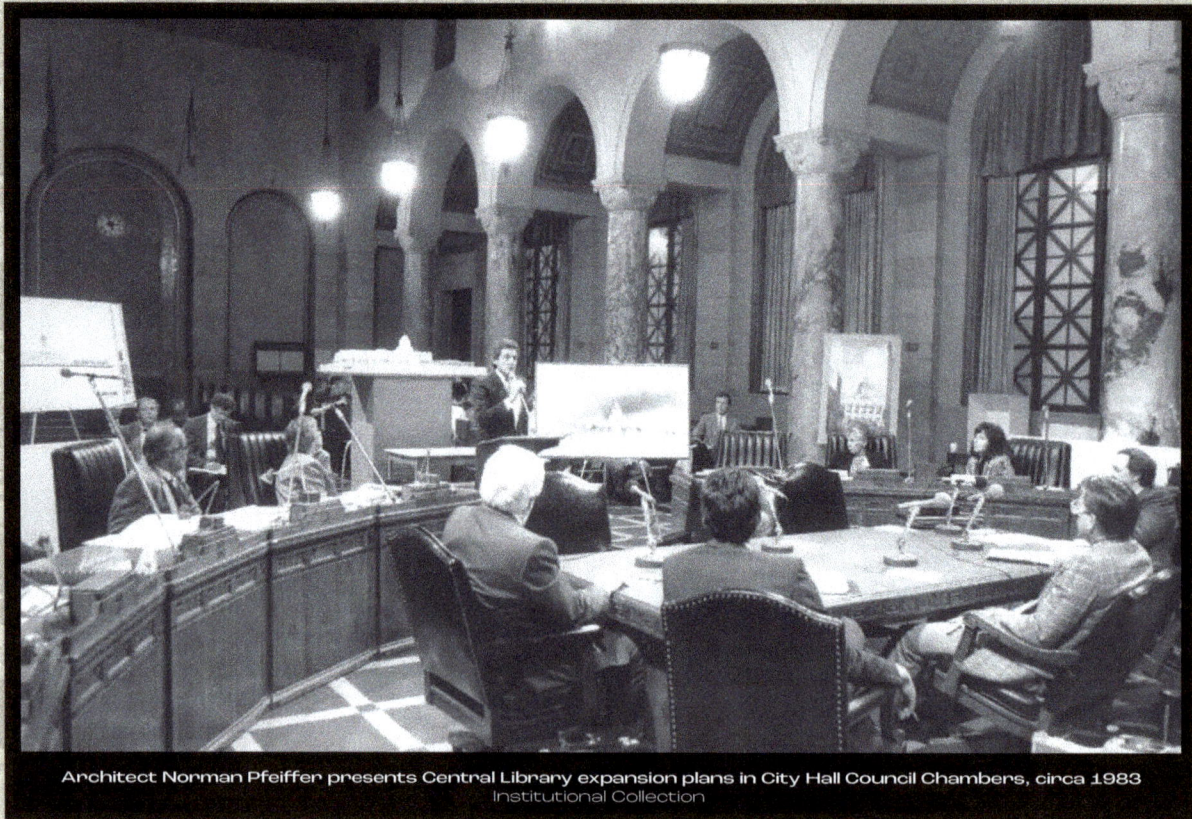

Architect Norman Pfeiffer presents Central Library expansion plans in City Hall Council Chambers, circa 1983
Institutional Collection

First Interstate World Center, under construction, looms over the Central Library, 1989
Paul Chinn, Herald Examiner Collection

The final expansion of Central Library was made possible by an innovative sale of "air rights." The space over the Central building was purchased to build the First Interstate Bank World Center, which became the tallest skyscraper in Los Angeles, located across 5th Street and still locally referred to as "the Library Tower." These funds ensured the expansion of Central Library, keeping the best of the old along with the new.

Etching of proposed Central Library Building, circa 1917

Dedicatory Exercises of the Central Library Building, 1926
Institutional Archive, Special Collections

Central Library: A Permanent Home at Last

For most of the Library's early history, it was unable to secure a permanent home. Through the dedicated efforts of the Library Board, the staff and the people of Los Angeles, funds were finally secured for a permanent central library building. On July 15, 1926, the building was dedicated. Library use in the new building increased immediately, and Central Library quickly became a cherished community space in downtown Los Angeles.

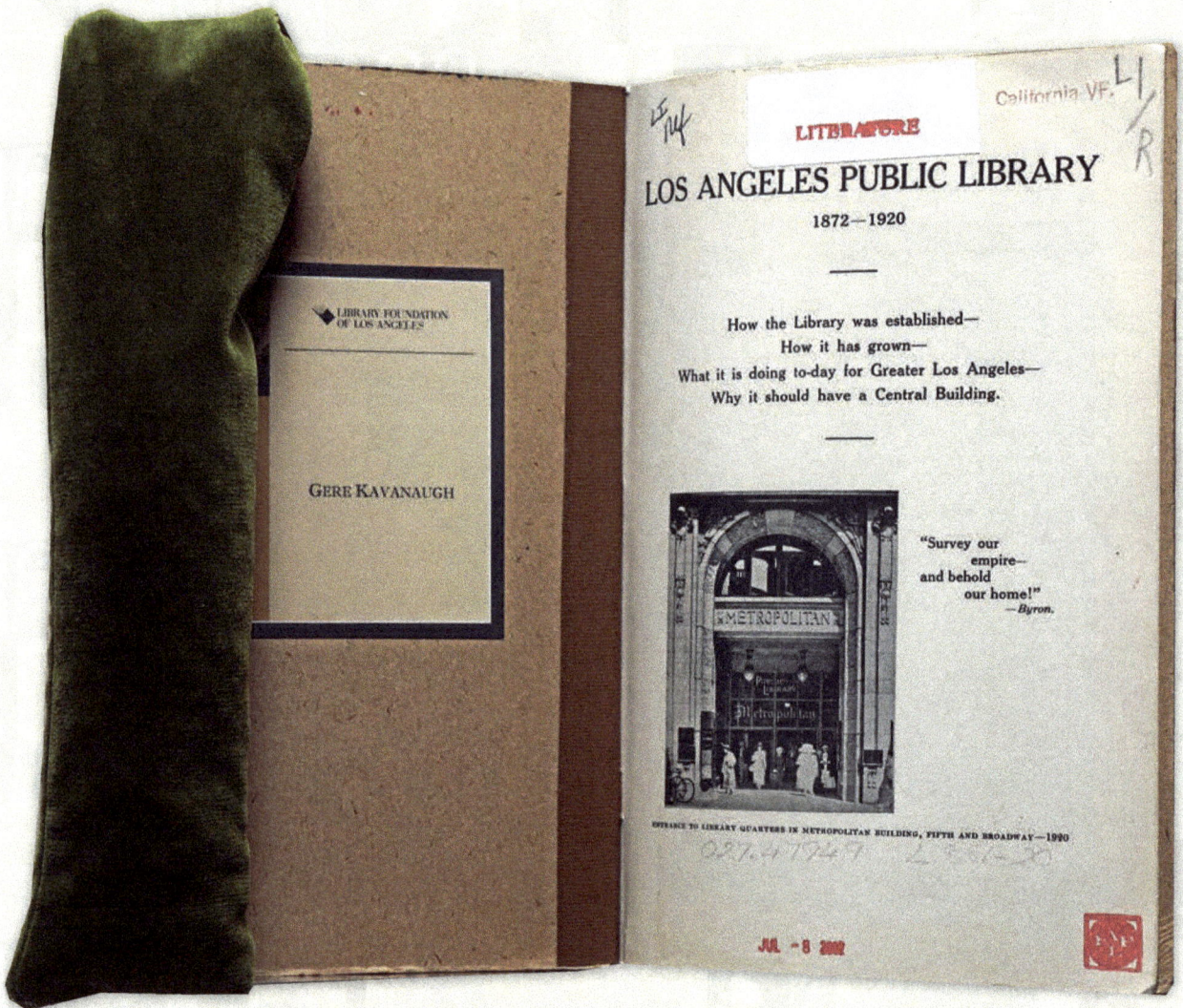

California VF.

LITERATURE

LOS ANGELES PUBLIC LIBRARY

1872—1920

How the Library was established—
How it has grown—
What it is doing to-day for Greater Los Angeles—
Why it should have a Central Building.

"Survey our
empire—
and behold
our home!"
—Byron.

ENTRANCE TO LIBRARY QUARTERS IN METROPOLITAN BUILDING, FIFTH AND BROADWAY—1920

How the Library was established—How it has grown—What it is doing to-day for Greater Los Angeles—Why it should have a Central Building, 1920
Institutional Archive, Special Collections

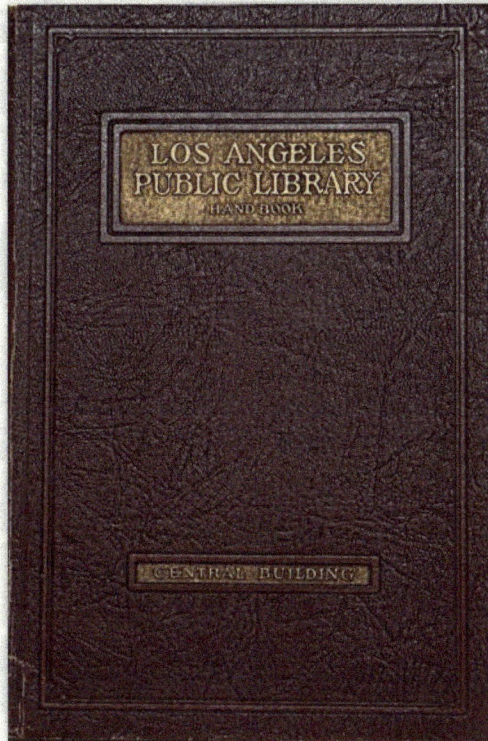

Hand Book of Central Building,
Los Angeles Public Library, 1927
Institutional Archive, Special Collections

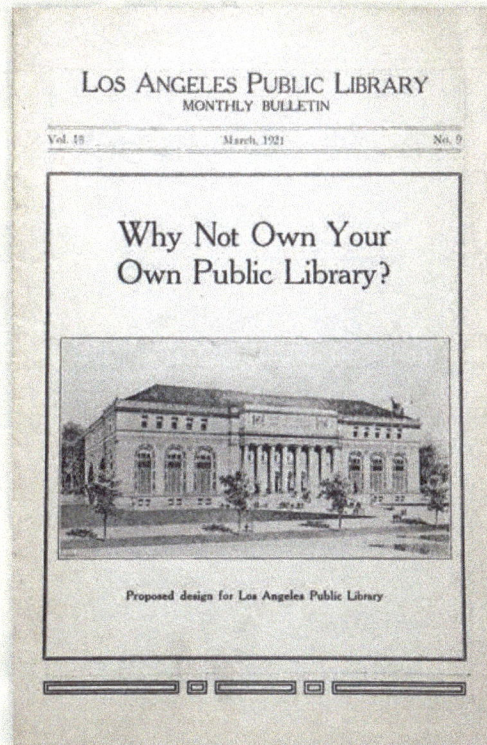

Los Angeles Public Library Monthly Bulletin, 1921
Institutional Archive, Special Collections

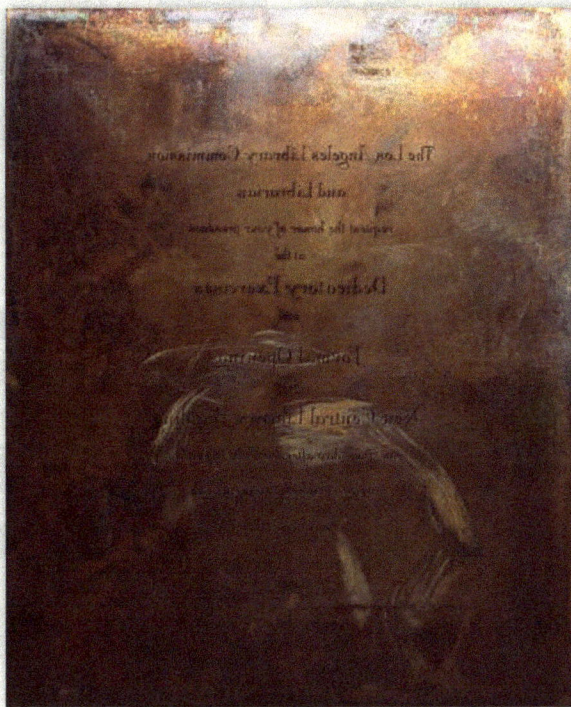

Central Library Formal Opening and Dedication, invitation and printing plate, 1926
Institutional Archive, Special Collections

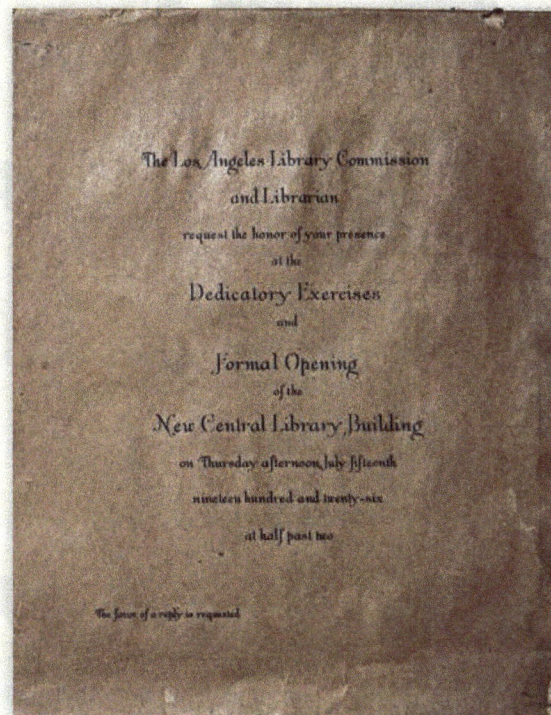

THE CENTRAL LIBRARY OF LOS ANGELES

A Report on the Present Building
(The Rufus B. von KleinSmid Central Library)
with Recommendations for a Facility
To Meet Service Requirements

Presented to the
Mayor and City Council of Los Angeles
by the

BOARD OF LIBRARY COMMISSIONERS

Los Angeles Public Library
December 1966

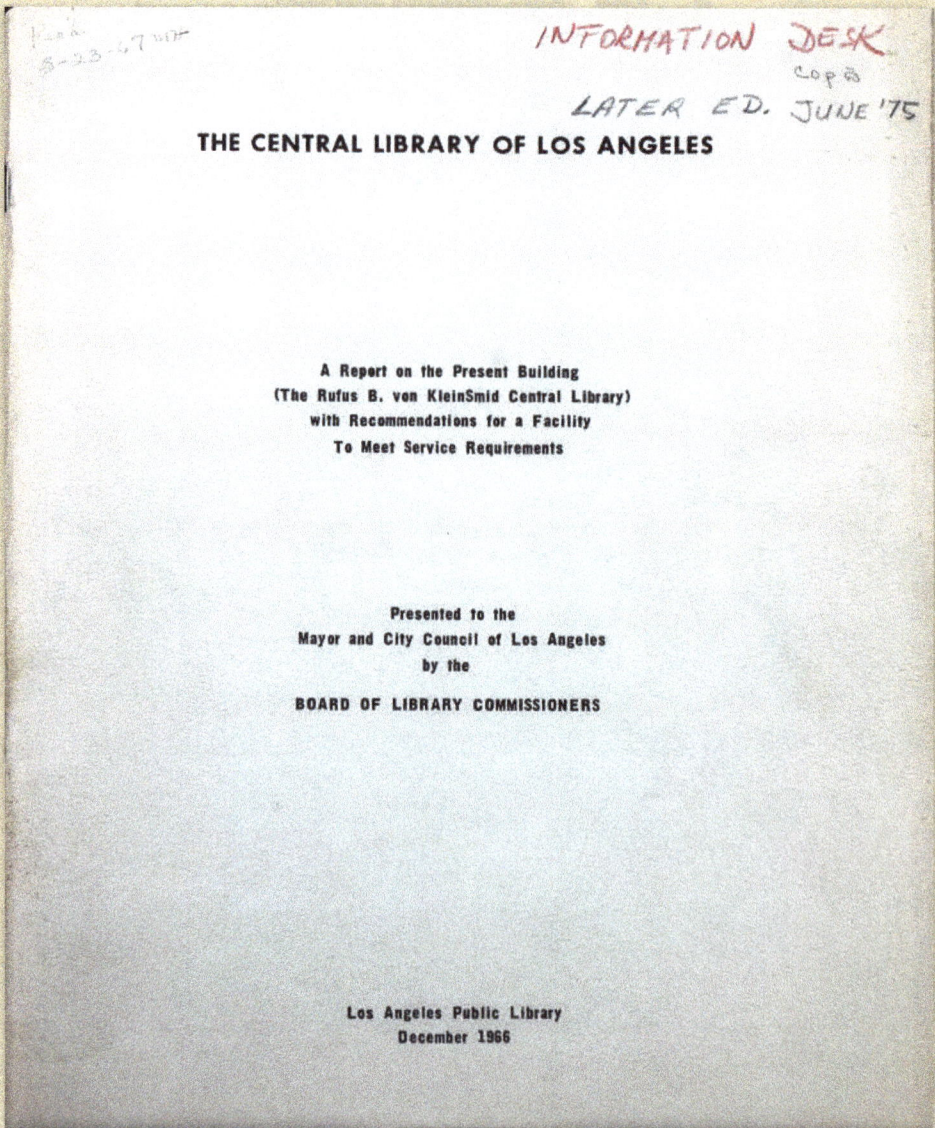

The Central Library of Los Angeles; a Report on the Present Building, aka "The Green Report," 1966
Literature & Fiction Department

"The Green Report" recommended demolition of the Goodhue building and construction of a new modern building on the same location. The report's recommendation was for an independent building to house the entire collection on the minimum number of floors with maximum square footage. The report was the official position of the Library Commissioners and supported by the majority of library staff who had to work in a building that suffered overcrowding, fire hazards and a lack of climate control.

The Central Problem

On opening, Central Library was the pride of downtown Los Angeles and a tourist destination. The astonishing growth of the city in the post-war years quickly overwhelmed the building's ability to assist all the library patrons who wanted to use it. In the age of midcentury modern, large open spaces were the model for libraries of the future. By contrast, the Central Library building was overcrowded, out of storage space, and a firetrap that lacked air conditioning. Library staff and administration were eager for a new building, and demolition plans were discussed in the late 1960s and 1970s. Central Library still had its supporters leading it to be placed on the National Register of Historic Places. The movement to save Central Library saw the birth of the Los Angeles Conservancy and a new movement to appreciate the architectural past of Los Angeles.

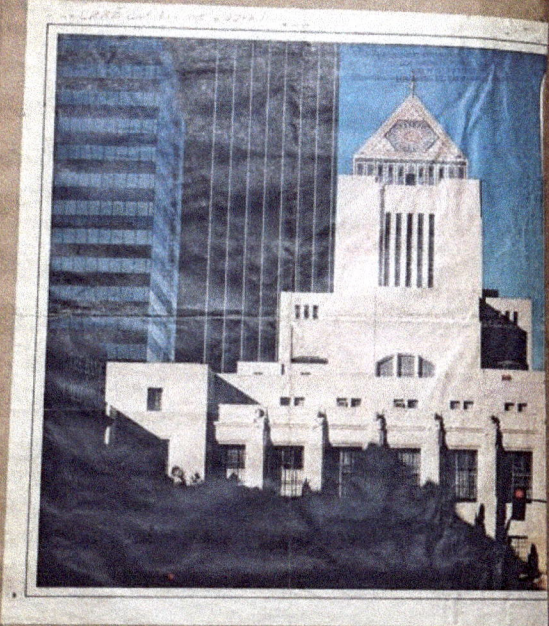

Central Library scrapbook, 1975–1984
Institutional Archive, Special Collections

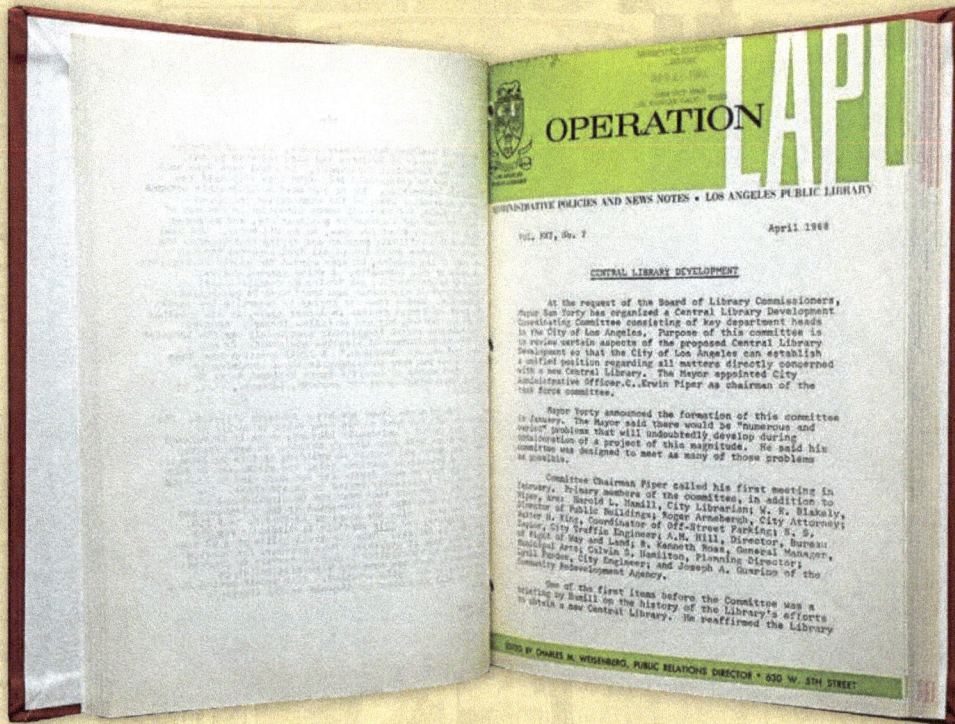

Central Library scrapbook, 1975-1984
Institutional Archive, Special Collections

CENTRAL LIBRARY TOUR GUIDE

LOS ANGELES, PUBLIC LIBRARY. TOURS.

LOS ANGELES PUBLIC LIBRARY

611—PUBLIC LIBRARY, LOS ANGELES, CALIFORNIA

Central Library postcard, undated
Institutional Archive, Special Collections

Central Library Tour Guide, brochure, undated
Institutional Archive, Special Collections

THE LOS ANGELES CONSERVANCY

News

"A Collector's Edition"

Vol. 1 No. 1

"A Collector's Edition"

Fall 1978

The LAC:
What We Are All About

Our Mission
The Los Angeles Conservancy dedicates itself to the protection and enhancement of the urban landscape of the Los Angeles region through the creation of a responsible, broadly representative voice for the conservation of our distinctive heritage of architecture and other urban forms.

Our Goals
To accomplish this mission, the Los Angeles Conservancy commits itself to three major goals.

Awareness: To increase public awareness of Los Angeles' irreplaceable historical, cultural, and architectural resources through a variety of activities; and to identify and strengthen a community of interest among existing groups and organizations.

Assistance: To provide a mutually supportive information network among the many and diverse urban conservation groups in the greater Los Angeles area; and to gather and disseminate information which can assist individuals and groups in the realization of specific projects involving the preservation of the urban environment.

Action: To encourage policies and decisions in the public and private sectors which recognize, conserve, and enhance the important features of Los Angeles' unique urban landscape; and to develop, as resources permit, a program of property and architectural easement acquisition.

Who We Are
Over the last year, many persons dedicated to protecting the built environment of the greater Los Angeles area have joined together to organize The Los Angeles Conservancy. Incorporation papers were filed in the spring of this year and application has been made for status as a tax-exempt organization.

The Conservancy is a membership organization, governed by a Board of Directors — currently numbering twelve — and assisted, in an advisory capacity only, by a distinguished Advisory Council.

President Margaret Bach, Advisory Board Member Kurt Meyer of FAIA, and Board Member David Workman (left to right) met the press to announce the birth of the LAC.

Board members are elected for two-year terms by the general membership at the Conservancy annual meetings held in May of each year. The Board meets more frequently, generally on a monthly basis, and Board meetings are open.

Key to the workings of the Conservancy are a number of active committees, including Program, Newsletter, Research, Fund-raising, Membership, Issue Task Forces, and a Speakers' Bureau.

What We Are Doing
In line with our commitment to become a positive force in the preservation and enhancement of the Los Angeles built environment, the Conservancy has — in the short time since its formation — begun to function in the following ways:

To promote **awareness:**
"Los Angeles Architecture: The Best Kept Secret in the West." With the generous assistance of Disney Productions, the Conservancy has produced a multi-media slide presentation about Los Angeles architecture which was premiered at the June fund-raiser at the Oviatt Building. The presentation will be utilized widely in future community programs.

The Los Angeles Conservancy News. Our quarterly newsletter represents an important element in our awareness campaign. It will become a vital tool to identify, build, strengthen, and inform the growing preservation constituency in

Los Angeles. The *News* will serve an equally important function in informing and educating public officials whose decisions affect, in a most profound way, the future of our urban environment.

Membership Meetings. Our periodic membership meetings are designed to inform and involve our membership in ongoing Conservancy activities and concerns.

Public Events. Once or twice a year, the Conservancy will sponsor public events designed to increase the public's awareness of the built environment. Our next event is scheduled for October 22 and will focus on the Broadway-Spring Street historic districts (see announcement, page 7).

To promote **assistance:**
Support Function. The Los Angeles Conservancy seeks to offer support and recognition of other Los Angeles groups sharing urban conservation goals. At the present time, the efforts of several groups are of particular interest and deserve special support. They are:

The Committee for Simon Rodia's Towers, which has persisted in its heroic efforts to keep the city's Watts Towers restoration on track in accordance with proper restoration techniques.

The Friends of the Schindler House, who are seeking funds for the purchase and

(Continued on pag

The Los Angeles Conservancy News, 1978
History & Genealogy Department, Periodicals Collection

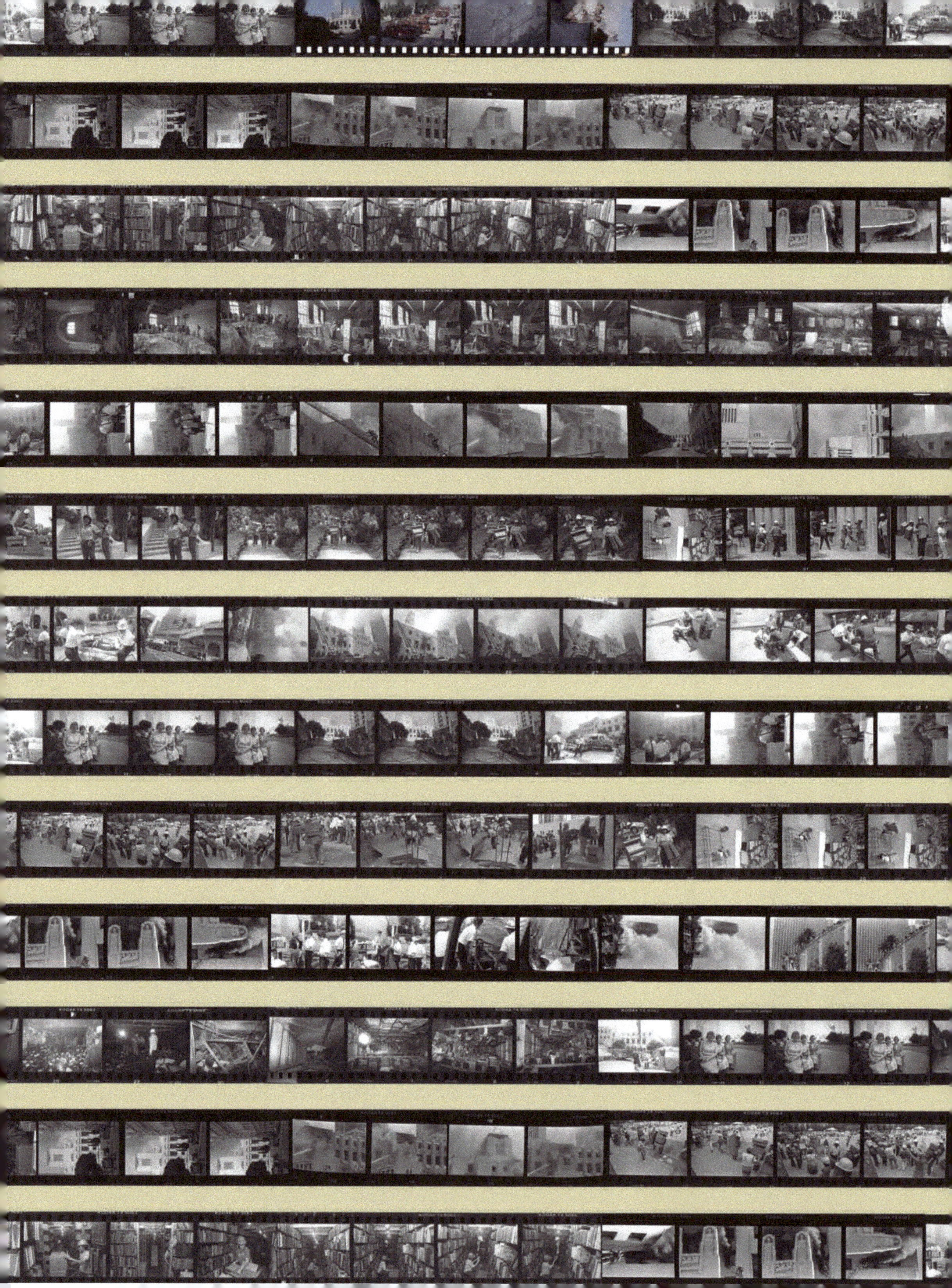

Central Library fire, 35mm negatives
Michael Haering, Leo Jarzomb, Javier Mendoza, Mike Mullen, 1986
Herald Examiner Collection

When the Central Library began to burn on April 29, 1986, multiple photographers from the *Los Angeles Herald Examiner* were dispatched to cover the events as they unfolded, along with the immediate aftermath and recovery. A small number of the images were printed and ran in the newspaper, leaving hundreds of exposures that have never been publicly exhibited until now.

THE CENTRAL LIBRARY FIRE
April 29, 1986

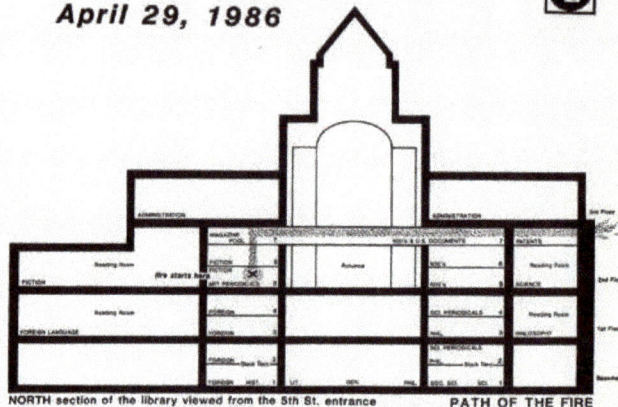

NORTH section of the library viewed from the 5th St. entrance   PATH OF THE FIRE

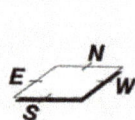

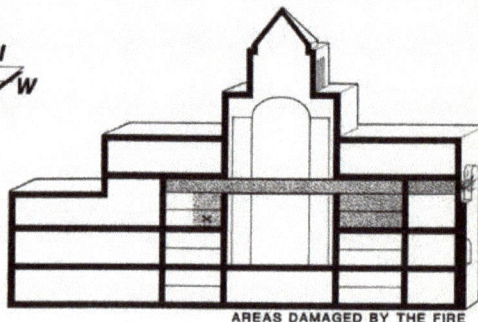

AREAS DAMAGED BY THE FIRE

Los Angeles Public Library

Diagram detailing path of
Central Library fire,
undated
Institutional Archive,
Special Collections

DUE TO THE APRIL 29 FIRE
THE CENTRAL LIBRARY IS CLOSED
TO THE PUBLIC

BOOKS MAY BE RETURNED
TO ANY BRANCH OF THE
LOS ANGELES PUBLIC LIBRARY

A TEMPORARY LOCATION FOR
THE CENTRAL LIBRARY WILL BE
ANNOUNCED AT A LATER DATE

Los Angeles Public Library

Sign noting the closure of
Central Library, 1986
Institutional Archive,
Special Collections

Recovering from Catastrophe

In the aftermath of the 1986 fire, the Central Library was closed. In an amazing sign of
community support, a volunteer crew of more than 1,700 people of all ages worked
24-hours-a-day to remove most of the books. Wet books were sent off to be freeze dried,
leaving hundreds of thousands of dry books that couldn't stay in the dusty, smoky building.
For more than a year afterward, staff worked in the scarred shell of Central Library,
inventorying and packing books onto pallets for transfer to warehouses east of downtown
at Rio Vista and Anderson streets. Staff did their best to organize and cultivate collections
while the search for a temporary Central Library proceeded.

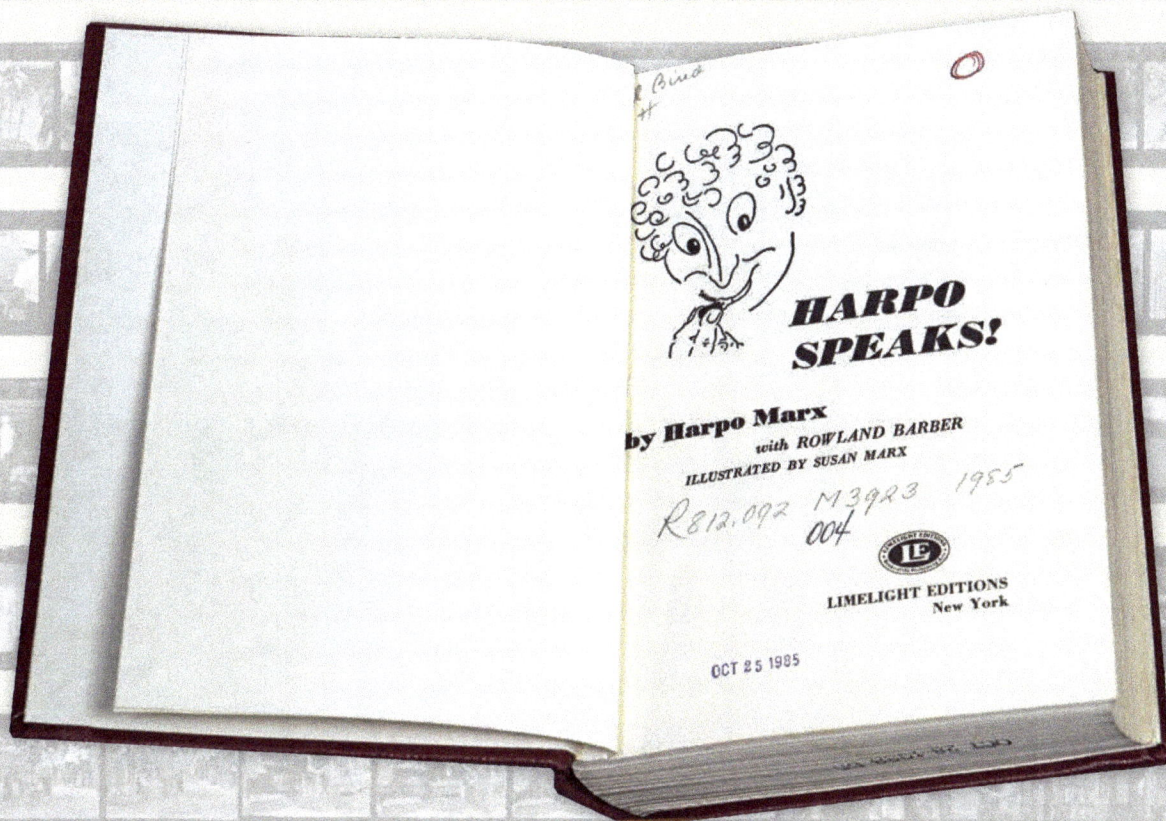

Red circular marking on title page of *Harpo Speaks* by Harpo Marx, 1985
Literature & Fiction Department

A Proclamation on the Move from
Los Angeles Central Library, 1987
Institutional Archive,
Special Collections

CENTRAL
L[I]
DECEM[BER]

Central Library staff and Library administration "Class" photo, taken eight months after the fire, 1986
Institutional Collection

T
BIG P
NAME

1. Helene Mochedlover (Literature/Fiction)
2. Judy Ostrander (Business/Economics)
3. Laurie Aron (Business/Economics)
4. Diane White (Branch Library Services)
5. Ken Jones (Business/Economics)
6. Glenda Prosser-Cohen (Business/Economics)
7. Kathy Scott (Business/Economics)
8. Marilyn Ayala (Business/Economics)
9. Bernadette Jones (Social Sciences)
10. David Gonnella (Social Sciences)
11. Jill Crane (Social Sciences)
12. Lois Bowman (Social Sciences)
13. Betty Shermer (GRS)
14. Catherine Lowry (Catalog)
15. Debra Stansberry (GRS)
16. Buffy Menter (Science/Technology)
17. Marianne Hart (Audio Visual)
18. Sandra Madden (Audio Visual)
19. Art Reynolds (Genealogy)
20. Dorothy Mewshaw (History)
21. Carolynn Germann (History)
22. Jane Nowak (Fiction)
23. Romaine Ahlstrom (Collection Development)
24. Evelyn Webb (Fiction)
25. Fumiko Terada (Science/Technology)
26. Mercy Webb (Science/Technology)
27. Margaret Lechuga (Science/Technology)
28. Tess Gan (Science/Technology)
29. Kenny Chiang (Fiction)
30. Linda Huynh (Science/Technology)
31. Marjorie Nelson (Science/Technology)
32. Dan Strehl (GRS)
33. Wendell Smith (Audio Visual)
34. Antar Mahmoud (Languages)
35. Rusty Balah (SCAN)
36. Ricardo Parada (Languages)
37. Bob Anderson (Literature/Fiction)
38. Judy Herman (SCAN)
39. Rick Wright (Security)
40. Joan Bartel (Administration)
41. Ruby Turner (Administration)
42. Laura Dwan (Science/Technology)
43. Ralph Colvin (Security)
44. Fred Durham (Security)
45. Henry Love (Shipping)
46. Stan Nobuta (Science/Technology)
47. Jim Aros (Science/Technology)
48. Johnny Slaughter (Science/Technology)
49. Erwin Lee (GRS
50. Glen Gonzales (Science/Technology)
51. Hee Jung Lee (Catalog)
52. David Clark (Photo Collection)
53. Betty Gay (Administration)
54. Tony Gutierrez (GRS)
55. Won Tak Kim (Catalog)
56. Violet Kuroki (Catalog)
57. Richard Partlow (Audio Visual)
58. Dorothy Wong (Catalog)
59. Noriel Ape (Business)
60. Kim Chang (Catalog)
61. Charmion Slaughter (Philosophy/Religion)
62. Choi Yan (Children's Literature)
63. Jeri Heckard (Art/Music)
64. Maggie Cabrera (Art/Music)
65. Bob Colwell (GRS)
66. Bob Patterson (Catalog)
67. Harry Sorensen (Catalog)
68. Loma Reynolds (Audio Visual)
69. Evelyn Greenwald (SCAN)
70. Marilyn Wherley (Social Sciences/Phil/Rel)
71. Richard Giannini (Philosophy/Religion)
72. David Moore (Social Sciences)
73. Linda Moussa (Social Sciences)
74. June Cheng (Languages)
75. Rolando Pasquinelli (Languages)
76. Ava Smith (Languages)
77. Anson Lee (Fiction)
78. Jackson Joe (Fiction)
79. Robert Lee (Genealogy)
80. Philips Panaligan (Literature)
81. Arthur Tam (GRS)
82. Helen Haskell (Science/Technology)
83. Donna Schneider (Patents)
84. Rolando Varela (GRS)
85. Gabriel Vasquez (GRS)
86. Alice Henninger (SCAN)
87. Lily Shintani (SCAN)
88. Russ Larcheveque (Security)
89. Eddis Hoffman (SCAN)
90. Paul Barkigia (Science/Technology)
91. Arnold Nunez (Science/Technology)
92. Isabel Lopez (Science/Technology)
93. Angela McDonald (Science/Technology)
94. Norberto Avina (Science/Technology)
95. Aida Pedroza (Science/Technology)
96. Thomas Gesinski (Audio Visual)
97. Mike Carroll (Audio Visual)
98. Lewis Williams (Audio Visual)
99. Merle Nunlee (Audio Visual)
100. Ruth Rowan (Audio Visual)
101. Tony Novoa (Literature)
102. Bob Day (Technical Services)
103. Choy Yan (Genealogy)
104. Tatiana Noscoff (Languages)
105. David Cerlian (Languages)
106. Sylva Manoogian (Languages)
107. Billie Connor (Science/Tech), holding
108. Bill Ybarra (GRS)
109. Guiomar Tamen (GRS)
110. Uy Gov (GRS)
111. Hy Tran (Catalog)
112. Betty Lum (Branch Library Services)
113. Oscar Ortiz (Business)
114. Mel Rosenberg (Art/Music)
115. Michael Uhlenkott (Public Relations)
116. Manny Medina (Public Relations)
117. Nona Crossman (Public Relations)

8. Michael Leonard (Public Relations)
9. Jack Vargas (Art/Music)
0. Carol Larson (Art/Music)
1. Dick Collins (Art/Music)
2. Wyman Jones (Administration)
3. Glen Creason (History)
4. Carlton Norris (ARCO)
5. Frank Louch (History)
6. Jaime Pulido (GRS)
7. Dorothy Weiss (Catalog)
8. Jennie Martinez (Catalog)
9. Lisa Brown (Catalog)
0. Edwina Jones (Catalog)
1. Debbie Swain (Catalog)
2. Lu Orlino (Catalog)
3. Dan Dupill (Audio Visual)
4. Becky Salazar (Telephone Operator)
5. Reba Harrison (GRS)
6. Sandra Daniels (GRS)
7. Rosalyn Rogers (Art/Music)
8. Mavis Brown (Custodian)
9. Marva Bright (GRS)
0. Elisa Gonzalez (Languages)
1. Ken Feder (Languages)
2. P.T.C. Bear
3. Maricruz Diaz (Languages)
4. Michael Kirley (Genealogy)
5. Pat Paternoster (Genealogy)
6. Rina Aragon (Social Sciences)
7. Mary Estrada (Social Sciences)
8. Gretchen Cooper (Catalog)
9. Sari Mittelbach (Catalog)
50. Gay Townsend (Catalog)
51. Ricardo Gregorio (Accounting)
52. Frank Knecht (Catalog)
53. Shirley Lockley (Catalog)
53. Sammie Doris Lockhart (Catalog)
54. Alice Myers (Catalog)
56. Betty Faye Brown (Catalog)

157. Shu Lien Chu (Business/Economics)
158. Jose Paiz (History)
159. Ruby Reza (Personnel)
160. Teresa Colten (Catalog)
161. Beverlee Kert (Collection Development)
162. Marilyn Bowlin (Collection Development)
163. Roselynn Lee (History)
164. Sheila Nash (Art/Music)
165. Linda Fink (Adult Services)
166. Antran Manoogian (Adult Services)
167. Jesse Angus (Accounting)
168. Rusty Arce (Accounting)
169. Lupe Santelices (Catalog)
170. Pat Ramirez (Catalog)
171. Carolyn Kozo (Photo Collection)
172. Ted Itagaki (History)
173. Pat Spencer (Social Sciences)
174. Carrie Lauer (History)
175. Carey Rowan (Social Sciences)
176. Nancy Uyemura (Social Sciences)
177. Raymond Lee (GRS)
178. Elsie Bowlen (GRS)
179. Gloria Stoudemire (GRS)
180. Mary Joe (GRS)
181. Miu Lei Tang (GRS)
182. Maria Novelo (GRS)
183. Ruth Holland (Science/Technology)
184. Lupe Villanueve (Literature)
185. Irma Vega (ILL)
186. Art Prado (Accounting)
187. Cindy Fong (Technical Services)
188. Jino Canizares (Technical Services)
189. Helen Murray (Science/Technology)
190. Kelly Luong (Technical Services)
191. Bridget Laday (GRS)
192. Scott Ross (History)
193. Shirley Rosen (Administration)
194. Susanna Silva (Science/Technology)
195. Mary Quon (Children's Services)

196. Priscilla Moxom (Children's Services)
197. Susan Patron (Children's Services)
198. Patricia Cazares (Children's Services)
199. Pat Zeidler (Science/Technology)
200. Robin Peshak (Adult Services)
201. Dorothy Helfeld (Children's Literature)
202. Maureen Wade (Children's Services)
203. Rosa Edwards (Children's Literature)
204. Renny Day (Children's Lit.), holding 205.
205. Santa Puppet
206. Bette McDonough (Art/Music)
207. Tom Owen (History)
208. Mathews Chakkanakuzhi(Photo Collection)
209. Joyce Albers (Photo Collection)
210. Gloria Barajas (History/Photo Collection)
211. Martha Ybarra (Photo Collection)
212. Cary Moore (GRS)
213. Keith Dasalla (GRS)
214. John Okabe (Technical Services)
215. Isabel Smith (Literature)
216. Jose Acosta (Investigator)
217. Anita Luna (Personnel)
218. Youssif Botros (Accounting)
219. Rose Reyes (Accounting)
220. Kay Gonzales (Personnel)
221. Elizabeth Rodriguez Barahona (Personnel)
222. Maricela Ortiz (Accounting)
223. Penny Rowland (Administration)
224. Aimee Knight (Accounting)
225. Luz Meras (Data Management Services)
226. Lilia Solis (Data Management Services)
227. Vinita Sharma (Data Management Services)
228. Barbara Hurr (Accounting)
229. Mary Pratt (History)
230. Carol Baldwin (Photo Collection)
231. Thelma Franz (Children's Literature)

Ablaze with Wit: Post-Fire Library T-shirts
In the aftermath of the devastating fire, the staff worked heroically under dire conditions to gather the undamaged books, well over a million, and pack them for transport. This involved three different moving phases: first, out of the library to temporary warehouses at Rio Vista and Anderson Street, then to Central Library's temporary location at the Design Center on Spring Street, and finally back to the renovated Central Library. Throughout this difficult time, Library staff kept their spirits up through puppet shows, performances of follies, and t-shirts that expressed their humor and spirit in dealing with extraordinarily difficult circumstances.

HELP
SAVE THE BOOKS
486-2140
L.A. CENTRAL LIBRARY

Save the Books Sphinx Bookends, Michael de Medina, 1986
Institutional Archive, Special Collections

Bookends in the form of Central Library's fabled sphinx statues were offered as part of the Save the Books fundraising campaign. The pewter versions were made available for purchase at the Save the Books store or via a mail order catalog. Donors who contributed more than $10,000 were given the black and gold pair, made of metal, with their name engraved on the back of the books, which were held in place with a magnet.

Save the Books!

The fire damage to the Central Library was enormous; nearly a half million books and other library items were lost. Lodsrick "Lod" Cook, the CEO of ARCO, which was headquartered in a neighboring skyscraper, witnessed the devastation firsthand and launched the Save the Books campaign to raise ten million dollars to replace books lost in the fire. A Save the Books gift shop was created with branded items available for purchase as an additional method of fundraising. Lod Cook and Mayor Tom Bradley helped form a Save the Books Blue Ribbon Committee, which is currently acknowledged on a plaque in the Central Library Rotunda. These fundraising efforts led to the establishment of the Library Foundation in 1992, which continues to support the Los Angeles Public Library.

400,000 BURN VICTIMS NEED YOUR HELP.

The fire at the Central Library was fact. Not fiction. On April 29th, 370,000 books went up in flames. On September 3rd, someone struck again, destroying thousands more. Gone are 90,000 science and technology books. 43,000 volumes of literature and fiction. Thousands of out of print novels. Countless pages will never be turned, unless you help. With your donation, we can replace the books. Read between the lines.

SAVE THE BOOKS

Please send your tax deductible check or money order in any amount you can afford to:
Save the Books, P.O. Box 1986, 515 S. Flower Street, Los Angeles, CA. 90071

Our thanks to Ron Avery Photography, Andresen Typographics and John Adams & Son Photoengraving.

Central Library

The **Central Library**

Los Angeles Public Library

Is *NOW OPEN* in its Temporary Location

433 S. SPRING ST.

Mon - Thu: 10 a.m. - 8 p.m.
Fri & Sat: 10 a.m. - 5:30 p.m.

Sign promoting temporary Central Library location, 1989
Institutional Collection

Spring Street Central Library, located inside the Title Insurance/Design Center Building, circa 1989
Institutional Collection

History & Genealogy Department, Design Center of Los Angeles, circa 1990
Cary Moore, Los Angeles Photographers Collection

During the recovery of Central Library, the staff and collections moved to a temporary location on multiple floors of a Spring Street office building where it operated for more than five years. The Library's branch system provided supplementary support for patrons and staff. As the reopening approached, the Los Angeles Public Library had its first and only float in the 1993 Rose Bowl parade to advertise the reopening later that year.

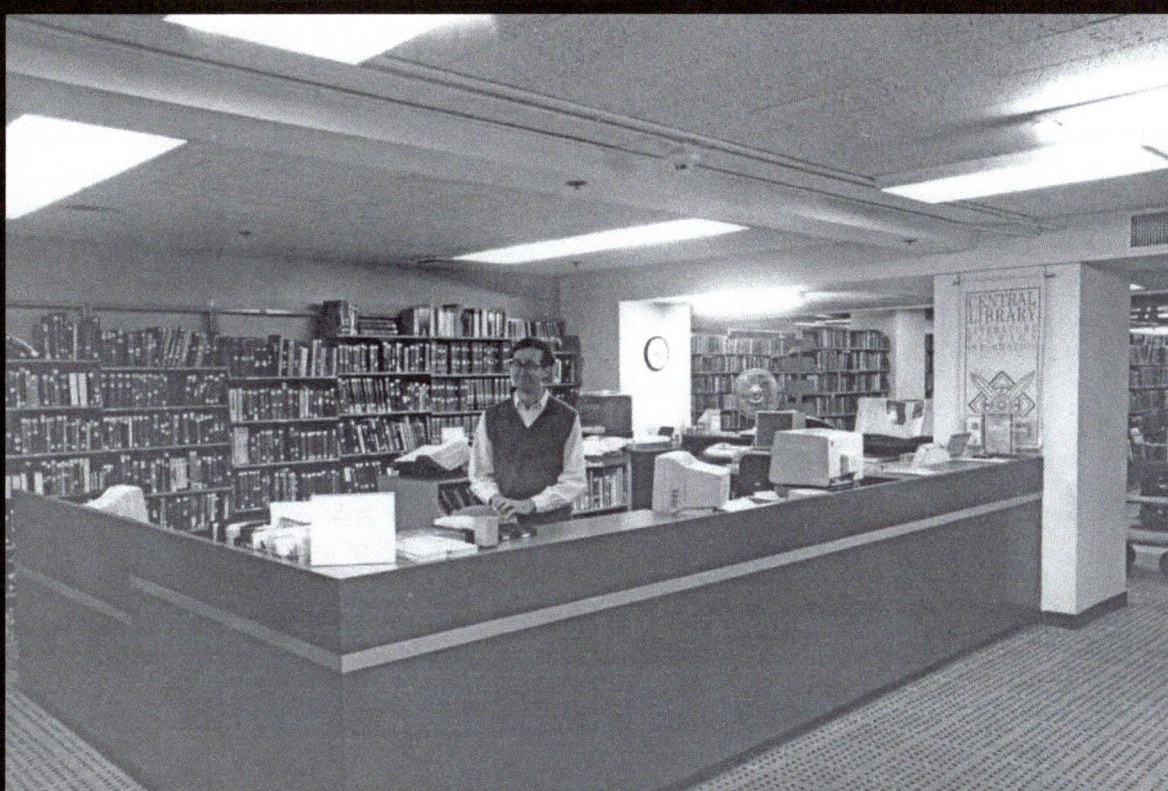

Literature & Fiction Department, Design Center of Los Angeles, circa 1990
Cary Moore, Los Angeles Photographers Collection

Business Department, Central Library at the Design Center of Los Angeles, circa 1990
Cary Moore, Los Angeles Photographers Collection

BOOKWORM

Los Angeles

Rendering of the Los Angeles Public Library's float for the 1993 Tournament of Roses parade
Institutional Collection

NOVEMBER 1993

AMERICAN LIBRARIES

Los Angeles Spectacular!

The city's new heart is its Central Library

INSIDE:

- Altruism factor
- IFLA & global access
- War for electronic turf
- Gay & lesbian archives
- Annual salary survey

Central Library featured on the cover of *American Libraries*, 1993

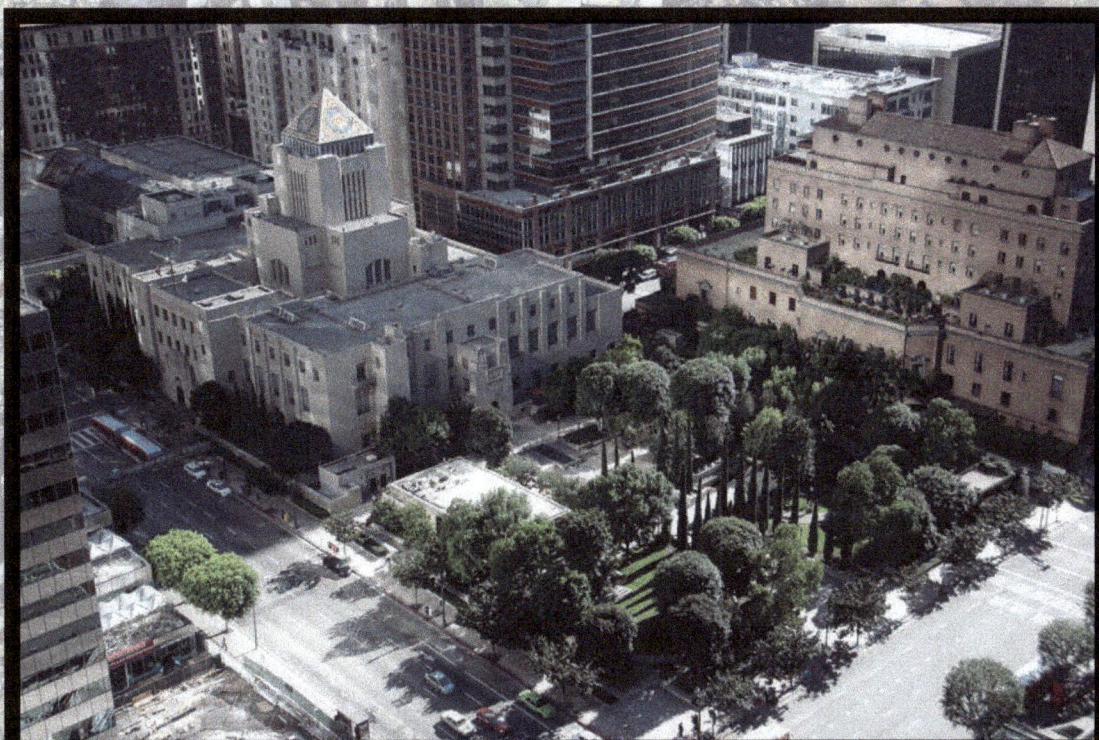

Aerial view of the expanded Central Library showing the reconstructed gardens, 2010
Gary Leonard, Institutional Collection

The Atrium of the Bradley Wing under construction, circa 1992
Institutional Collection

View of the Atrium in 2010
Gary Leonard, Institutional Collection

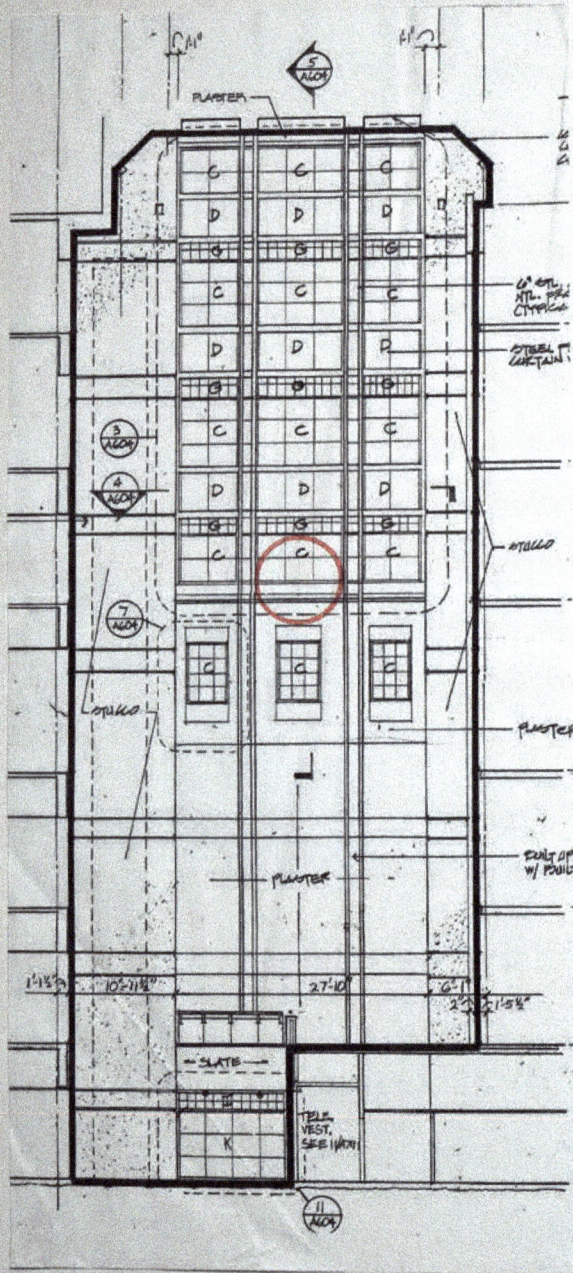

Proposed Central Library artwork,
Stephen Prina, 1989
Institutional Archive, Special Collections

In a nod to Goodhue's intent,
Architect Norman Pfeiffer
integrated art into the design
of the added wing. However, a
number of public art proposals
were never realized due to
lack of funds. These included
a massive tile-and-plaster
design for the entire south
wall of the atrium; three
murals; portals for the library's
seven departments, using
photographs, transparencies
and text; and last and not least,
a clock that would use hourly
chimes based on Billboard-
charted pop songs. It was not
determined whether these
songs would change over the
years or if October 1993 would
be aurally enshrined at Central
Library for all time.

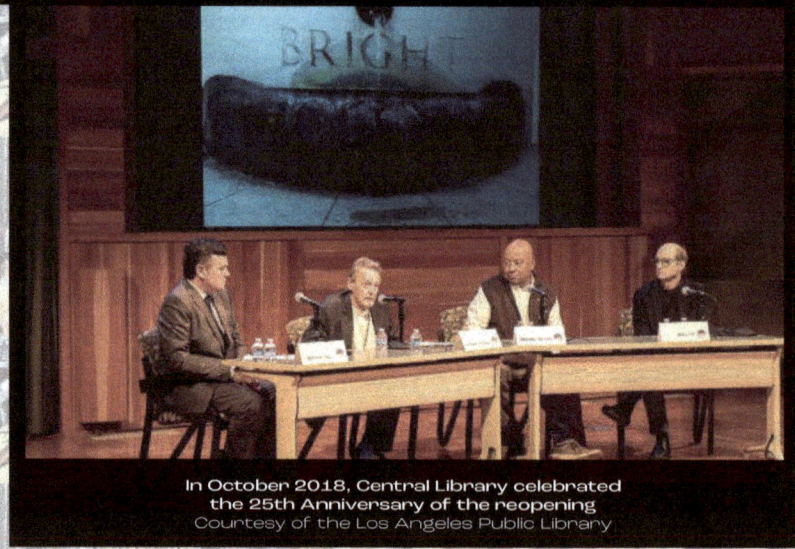

In October 2018, Central Library celebrated
the 25th Anniversary of the reopening
Courtesy of the Los Angeles Public Library

At last the new Central Library opened its doors, and Library staff returned to an expanded, brighter home, with the Subject Departments now housed on completely new and much larger floors, and joined through a soaring atrium. Public art adorned the new spaces, notably the atrium chandeliers and lamps. The new building was joyously received by Angelenos, so much so that a 25th anniversary celebration of the reopening was a huge success.

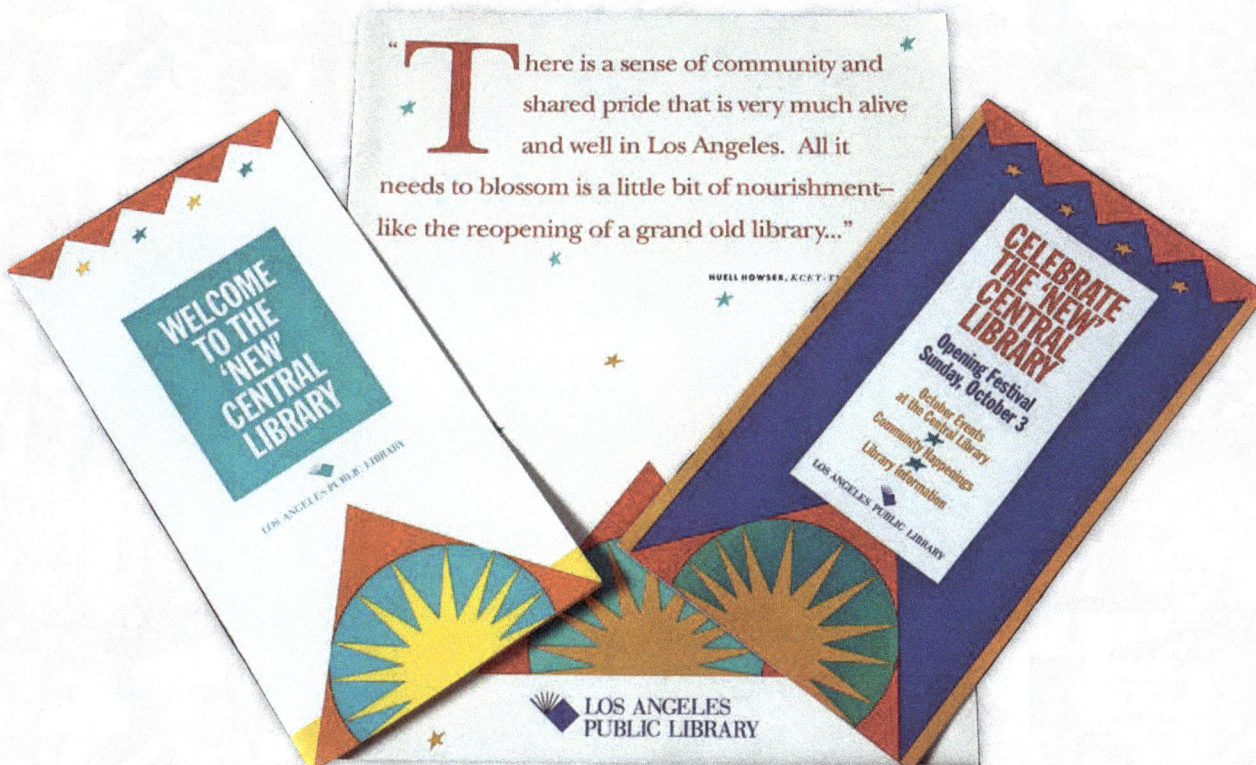

"There is a sense of community and shared pride that is very much alive and well in Los Angeles. All it needs to blossom is a little bit of nourishment—like the reopening of a grand old library..."

HUELL HOWSER, KCET-TV

WELCOME TO THE 'NEW' CENTRAL LIBRARY

LOS ANGELES PUBLIC LIBRARY

CELEBRATE THE 'NEW' CENTRAL LIBRARY

Opening Festival
Sunday, October 3

October Events
at the Central Library

Community Reopenings

Library Information

LOS ANGELES PUBLIC LIBRARY

LOS ANGELES PUBLIC LIBRARY

LEFT: *Welcome to the 'New' Central Library*, brochure, 1993
CENTER: Commemorative of Central Library's reopening, 1993 · Special Collections
RIGHT: Celebrate the 'New' Central Library, printed calendar of events, 1993
Institutional Archive, Special Collections

Reopening a Renovated and Expanded Central Library

The absence of Central Library for many years made the reopening so much sweeter. The outpouring of love for the Library from Los Angeles residents was matched by the happiness of the staff to return to their home after wandering near and far. The "new Central" was actually two buildings connected to each other: the Goodhue original and the Bradley Wing, with most of the collections and reference staff located in the new annex. Central Library was back and better than ever, and the public was so appreciative that the 25th anniversary of its reopening was wildly successful.

Welcome to the 'New" Central Library brochure, 1993
Art, Music & Recreation Department

THE BOARD OF LIBRARY COMMISSIONERS

Invites you to
Groundbreaking Ceremonies
for the

Rehabilitated and Expanded

CENTRAL LIBRARY

Los Angeles Public Library
630 West Fifth Street
Los Angeles, California

Friday, June 3, 1988
2:30 P.M.

Tom Bradley
Mayor

Gilbert W. Lindsay
Councilman, 9th District

Central Library groundbreaking invitation, 1988
Institutional Archive, Special Collections

Commemorative Central Library t-shirt, 1993
Institutional Archive, Special Collections

Staff giveaways for Central 25 celebration, 2018
Institutional Archive, Special Collections

Serving the City

Bookmobile interior, circa 1949
Institutional Collection

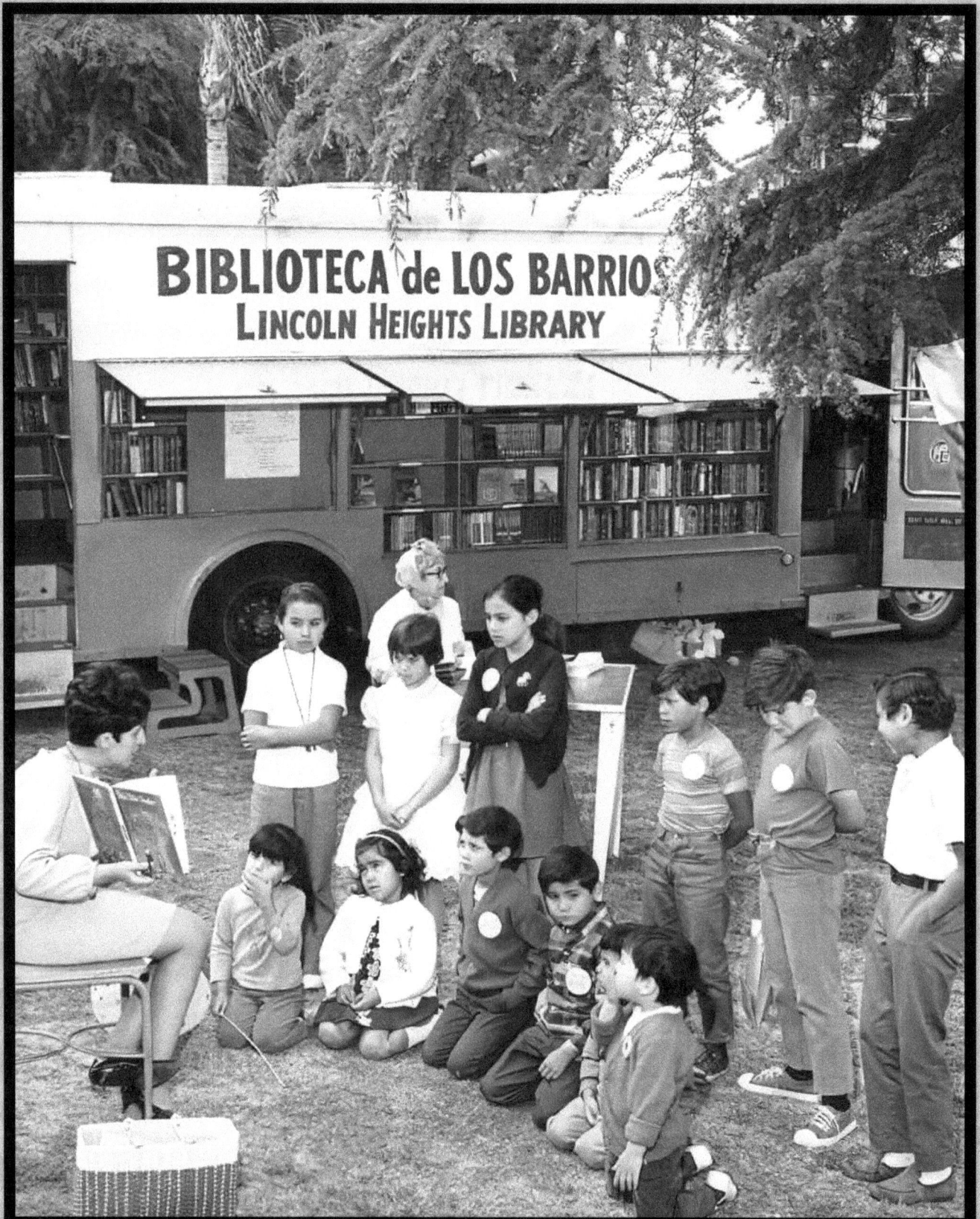

Storytime outside the Lincoln Heights Bookmobile, 1964
Institutional Collection

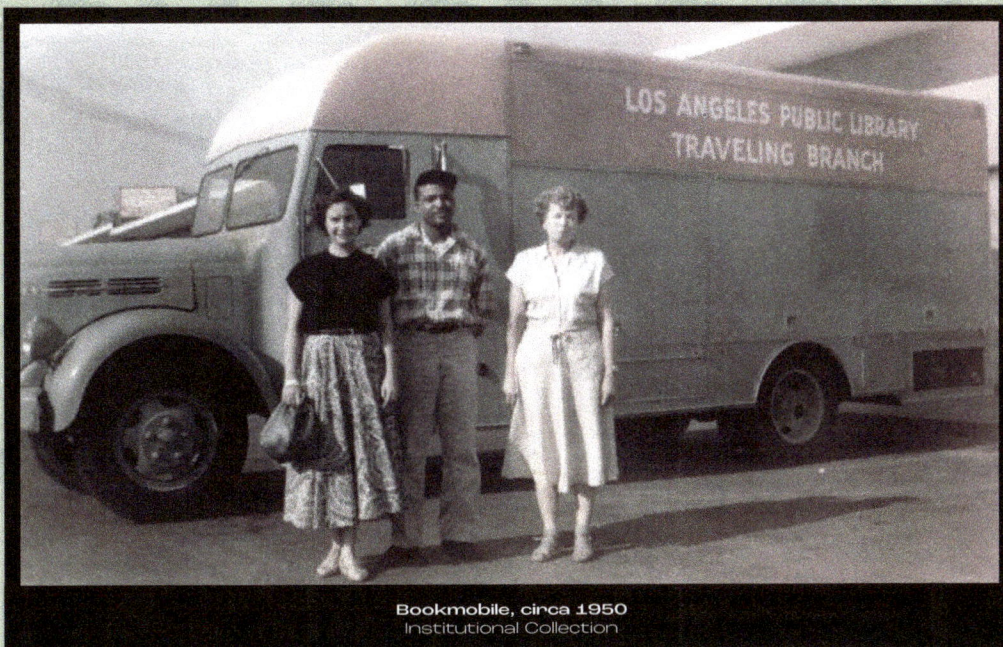

Bookmobile, circa 1950
Institutional Collection

Decorated Bookmobile, circa 1955
Joe Friezer, Institutional Collection

The Library's historical function has been to get books into the hands of its residents. In the past, the first interaction with the Library for many people were its bookmobiles. The postwar population boom meant that many new neighborhoods didn't have branch libraries. Bookmobiles provided a popular and flexible answer. From 1949 to 2004, Los Angeles Public Library's "Traveling Branches" brought library services to neighborhoods where branch libraries had not yet been established. Adult bookmobiles helped bring services to the postwar influx of veterans to the City, especially in the San Fernando Valley.

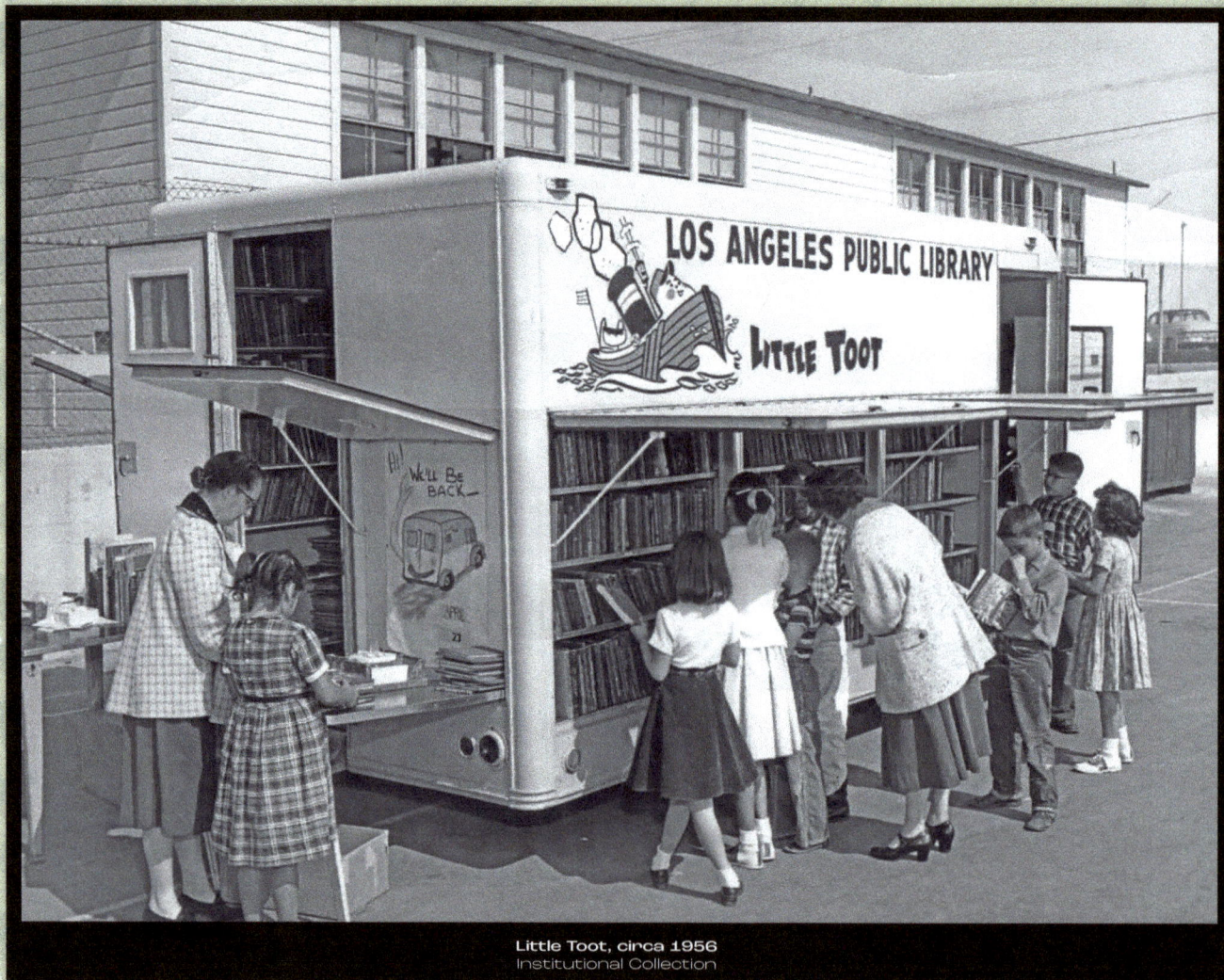

Little Toot, circa 1956
Institutional Collection

Childrens' bookmobiles proved very popular, and Little Toot was the favorite of many. Based on the children's book of the same name, its collection included approximately 3,000 books for students from kindergarten through the eighth grade. It served 27 schools, and its success led to more bookmobiles serving L.A.'s youngest patrons.

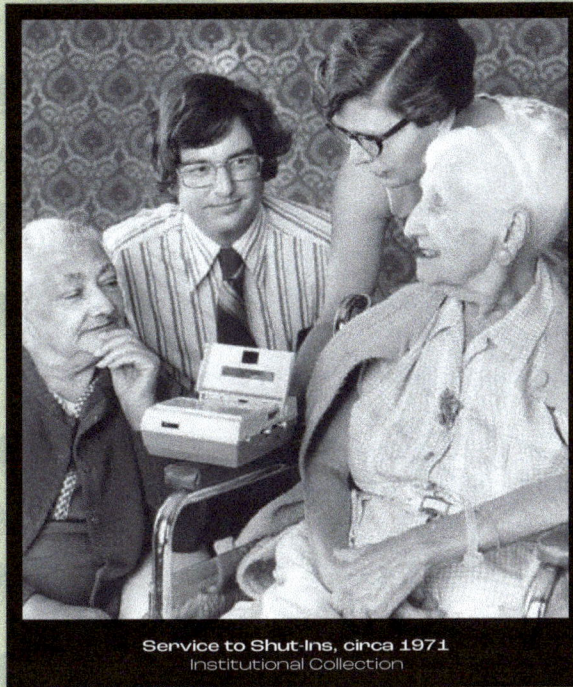

Service to Shut-Ins, circa 1971
Institutional Collection

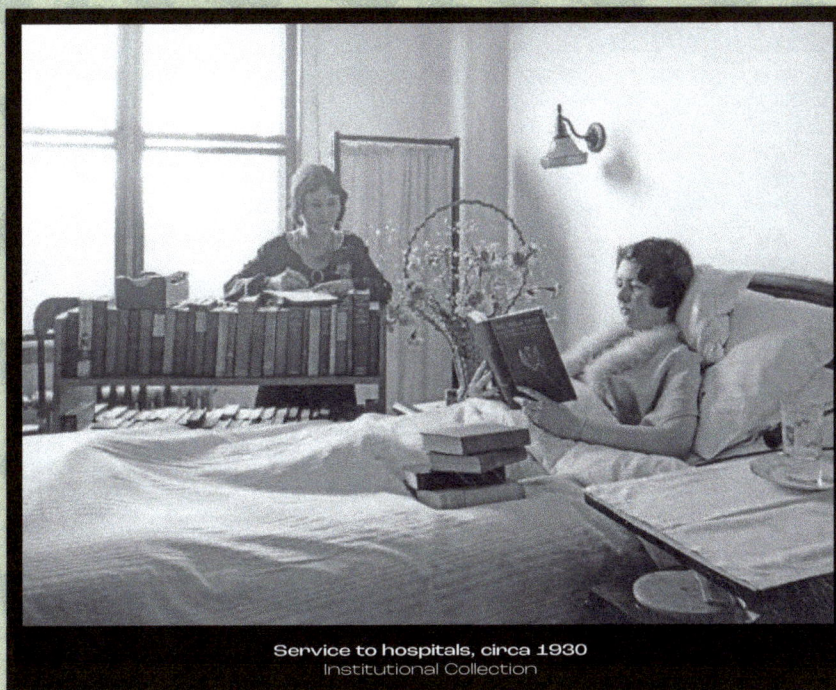

Service to hospitals, circa 1930
Institutional Collection

The Los Angeles Public Library has a long history of bringing books and library materials to those who are unable to come to the library. Services to hospitals was an early example, and other medical institutions were also favored by the Library's outreach services. A later example was the very successful Service to Shut-Ins, which directly connected librarians with community members in their homes. Volunteers have continued to serve as one of the Library's most significant assets in this and many other programs.

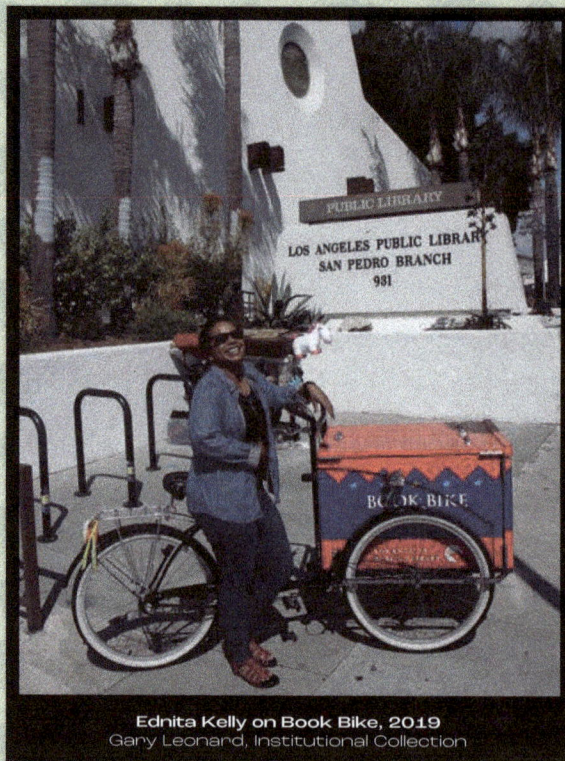

Ednita Kelly on Book Bike, 2019
Gary Leonard, Institutional Collection

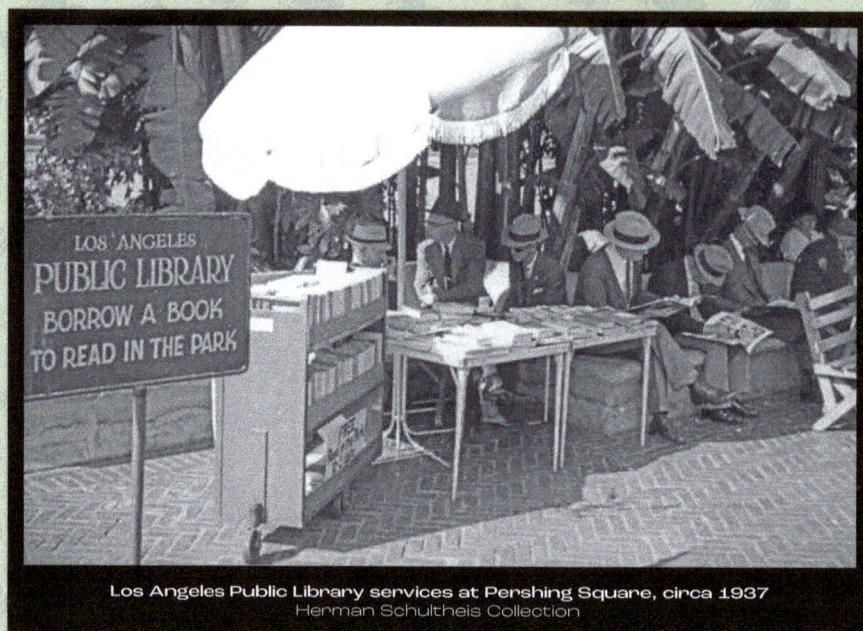

Los Angeles Public Library services at Pershing Square, circa 1937
Herman Schultheis Collection

The Library's staff members have a history of being flexible in meeting patrons where they are. During the Great Depression, Los Angeles Public Library operated out of a mobile table in Pershing Square, offering books and library cards. A more modern version of this is the Book Bike, which offers books and library cards. The Book Bike was inaugurated at the San Pedro Branch Library and has appeared at events across the City, introducing the Library and its services to people who are not regular patrons.

A LIBRARY of LANGUAGES

ARABIC	ܡܰܟܬܒ̇ܐ
ARMENIAN	գրադարան
CHINESE	圖書館
CZECH	knihovna
DANISH	bibliotek
DUTCH	bibliotheek
FINNISH	kirjasto
FRENCH	bibliothèque
GERMAN	Bibliothek
GREEK	βιβλιοθήκη
HEBREW	ספריה
HUNGARIAN	könyvtár
ITALIAN	biblioteca
JAPANESE	図書館
KOREAN	도서관
LATVIAN	biblioteka
LITHUANIAN	biblioteka
NORWEGIAN	bibliotek
PERSIAN	کتابخانه
PILIPINO	aklatan
POLISH	biblioteka
PORTUGUESE	biblioteca
RUSSIAN	библиотека
SERBO-CROATIAN	книжница
SPANISH	biblioteca
SWEDISH	bibliotek
VIETNAMESE	Thư-viện
YIDDISH	ביבליאטהעק

Over 170,000 books & periodicals in 28 languages spoken all over the world are available in the department and through local branch libraries. Reference, interpretation and translation services are provided by multilingual staff.

Foreign Languages Department
CENTRAL LIBRARY
LOS ANGELES PUBLIC LIBRARY
630 West Fifth Street
Los Angeles, California 90071
Telephone: (213) 620-7561 Ext. 291
612-3291

A Library of Languages, handout, undated
Institutional Collection, Special Collections

Los Angeles Public Library has a venerable tradition of providing books and periodicals in other languages. In the early days of the system, directional signs in some branches were written in different languages, and the collection offered books in many other languages in an attempt to provide services and representation for L.A.'s many immigrant communities. As early as the 1930s, the Library offered lectures featuring speakers in languages other than English, attracting many non-English speakers to the library. Today the Library offers literature, poetry, drama, history, biography, fiction, magazines and newspapers in as many as 30 different languages, and some branches have collections directed towards the language needs of the neighborhoods they serve.

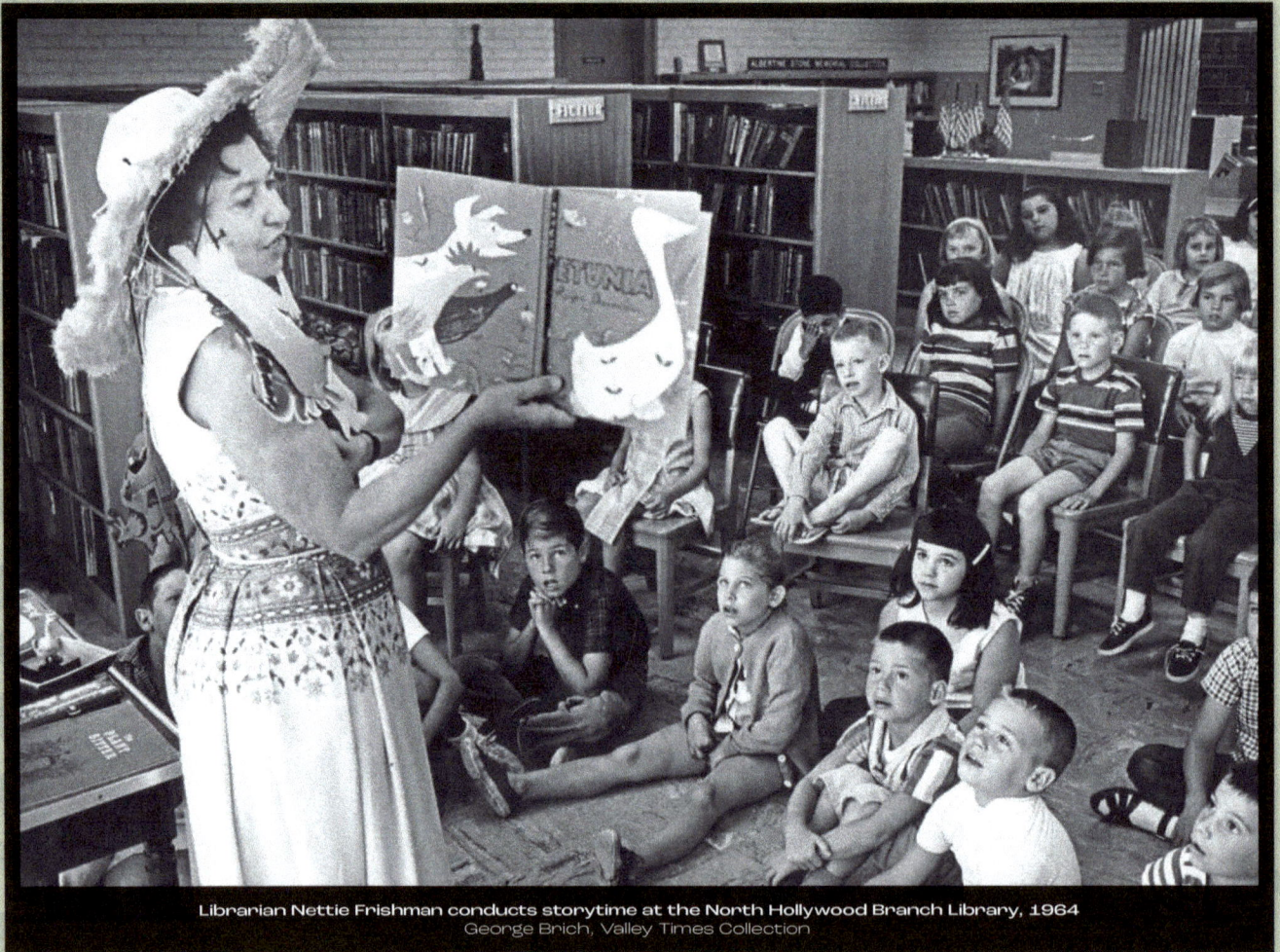

Librarian Nettie Frishman conducts storytime at the North Hollywood Branch Library, 1964
George Brich, Valley Times Collection

The Library has a long history of reaching beyond its four walls into neighborhoods and communities. Providing services to children is one of the oldest areas of outreach dating back to when the Los Angeles Public Library provided books for the City's classrooms. Today the first experience many Angelenos have with the Library is during a school visit conducted by an enthusiastic librarian.

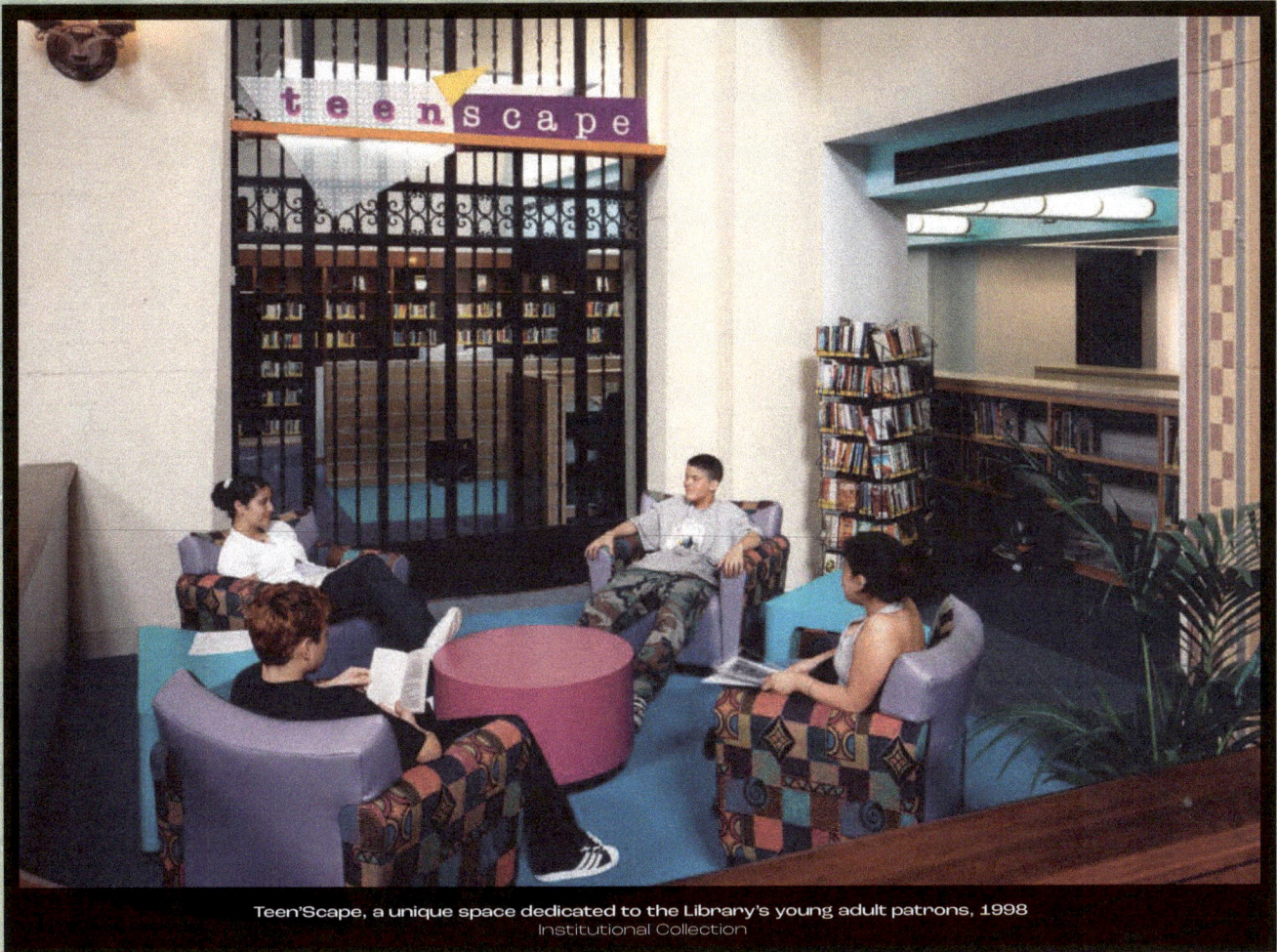

Teen'Scape, a unique space dedicated to the Library's young adult patrons, 1998
Institutional Collection

Teen Services focuses on reaching a population who might not realize that there are library resources designed just for them. An example of this is the "library within the library" of Teen'Scape. Celebrating its twenty-fifth anniversary this year, Teen'Scape is the very first public library space dedicated to teens, providing them with a place of their own to study, read, and relax.

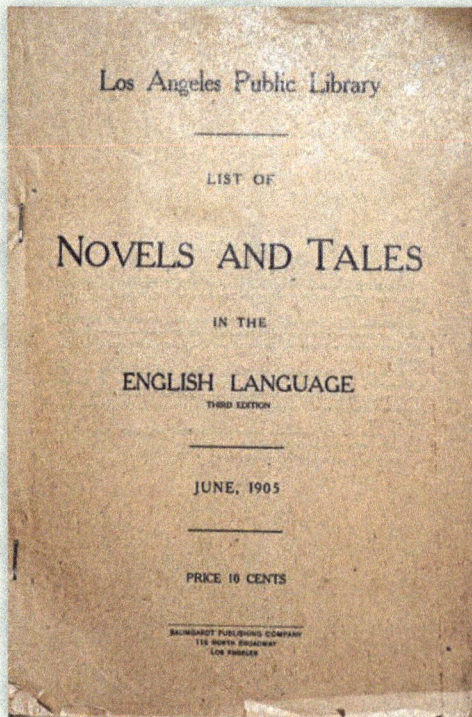

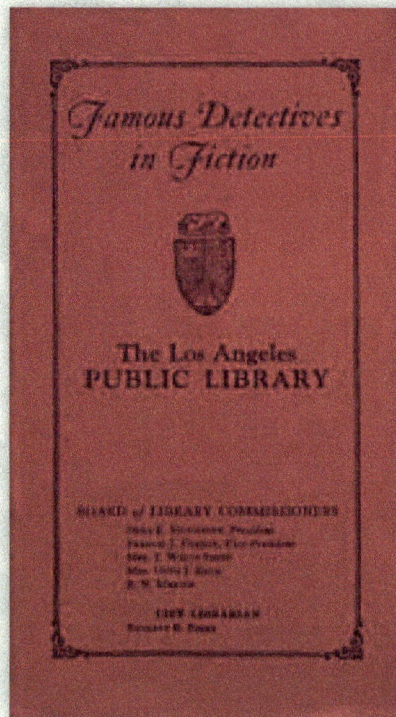

"What Should I Read?"

For most of their history, the main job of libraries has been bringing together books with readers of all ages. This matchmaking has served many purposes for patrons, from education to recreation to social awareness. Book lists have been a big part of what librarians call "Readers Advisory" which answers the perennial question: "What should I read?"

YOUR LIBRARY CAN HELP YOU . . .

EFFECTIVE LIVING

Philosophy and Religion
Department
Los Angeles
Public Library
1931

LIBRARY COMMISSION

ORRA E. MONNETTE
FRANCIS J. CONATY
MRS. J. WELLS SMITH
MRS. OTTO J. ZAHN
B. H. MARTIN

CITY LIBRARIAN
EVERETT R. PERRY

Family History
Aids to genealogical research

GENEALOGY ROOM

HISTORY DEPARTMENT

LOS ANGELES PUBLIC LIBRARY
630 W. FIFTH STREET
LOS ANGELES, CALIF. 90071
(213) 612-3317

Hours of Service
Monday through Thursday
10 a.m. to 8 p.m.
Friday and Saturday
10 a.m. to 5:30 p.m.

HOURS MAY BE SUBJECT TO CHANGE

Gifts to the Genealogy Division
are welcomed

CALIFORNIA

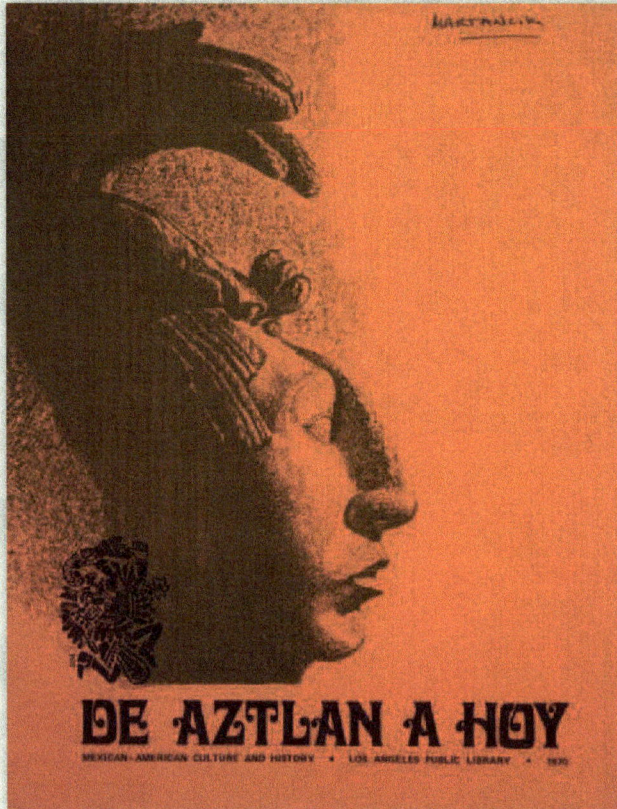

DE AZTLAN A HOY

MEXICAN-AMERICAN CULTURE AND HISTORY • LOS ANGELES PUBLIC LIBRARY • 1970

Skilful Parents

A list of books selected by:
The Los Angeles Public Library

The Guiding Parent continued

Special Topics

For Parents and their Children

LOS ANGELES PUBLIC LIBRARY

YOUR PREJUDICE IS SHOWING!

American Brotherhood Week Feb. 22-29

Sponsored by the National Conference of Christians and Jews in cooperation with community groups of all races and creeds.

The Los Angeles Public Library suggests these books for your American Brotherhood Week reading.

Baruch, Dorothy
Glass House of Prejudice

Boas, Franz
Race and Democratic Society

Bontemps, Arna
They Seek a City

Conrad, Earl
Jim Crow America

Crum, B. C.
Behind the Silken Curtain

Gordon, Alvin
Our Son Pablo

Faulkner, William
Intruder in the Dust

Gandhi, M. K.
Autobiography

Gordon, Alvin
Our Son Pablo

Griffith, Beatrice
American Me

Loescher, F. S.
Protestant Church and the Negro

MacIver, R. M.
Unity and Difference in American Life

McWilliams, Carey
North from Mexico

Miller, Arthur
Focus

Moon, Bucklin
The High Cost of Prejudice

Nelson, W. S., ed.
Christian Way in Race Relations

Northrop, F. S.
Meeting of East and West

Ojike, Mbonie
I Have Two Countries

Paton, Alan
Cry the Beloved Country

Petry, Ann
The Street

Rose, Arnold and Caroline
America Divided

Shaw, Irwin
Young Lions

Public Library
Board of
Library Commissioners

Christmas
Material

Found in the
Los Angeles Public Library

Philosophy and Religion Department
LOS ANGELES PUBLIC LIBRARY
Los Angeles, California

Libros Bilingües

Traducciones y Libros Recomendables

Bilingual books, translations and recommended books in Spanish.

Compiled by José G. Taylor

CHILDREN'S SERVICES

Los Angeles Public Library

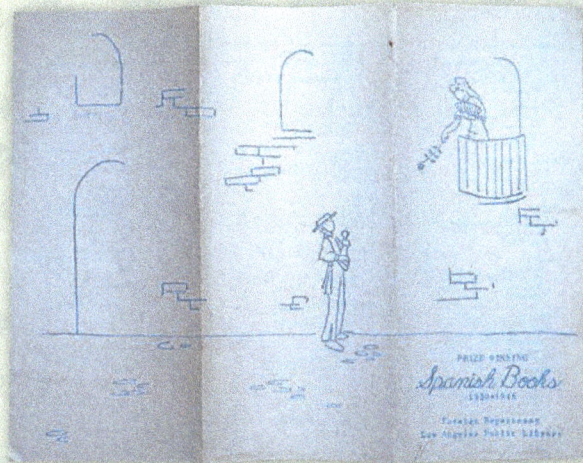

PRIZE WINNING
Spanish Books

Gaining An Understanding

301.4157 B658 — Blumenfeld, Warren. *Looking at Gay and Lesbian Life.* 1989.

301.4157 C678 — Cohen, Susan. *When Someone You Know Is Gay.* 1989.

301.4157 C799 — Corley, Rip. *The Final Closet: The Gay Parents' Guide for Coming Out to Their Children.* 1990.

301.4157 F815 — Fairchild, Betty. *Now That You Know: What Every Parent Should Know About Homosexuality.* 1989.

301.4157092 F897 — Fricke, Aaron. *Reflections of a Rock Lobster: A Story About Growing Up Gay.* 1981.

301.4157 G851 — Griffin, Carolyn. *Beyond Acceptance: Parents of Lesbians & Gays Talk About Their Experiences.* 1990.

616.9704 K88 — Kramer, Larry. *Reports from the Holocaust: The Making of an AIDS Activist.* 1989.

301.4157 M6495 — Miller, Neil. *In Search of Gay America: Women and Men in a Time of Change.* 1989.

301.4157 M958 — Muller, Ann. *Parents Matter: Parents' Relationships with Lesbian Daughters and Gay Sons.* 1987.

Gaining An Understanding

NEW — Rooke, Janice. *Understanding Sexual Identity: A Book for Teens and Their Friends.* 1990.

301.4157 T3985 — *There's Something I've Been Meaning to Tell You.* 1989.

Historical Perspective

301.4157 D815 — Duberman, Martin. *About Time: Exploring the Gay Past.* 1986.

301.4157 I76 — Isay, Richard. *Being Homosexual: Gay Men and Their Development.* 1989.

301.4157 K19 — Katz, Ned. *Gay American History: Lesbians and Gay Men in the USA.* 1985.

301.4157 P713 — Plant, Richard. *Pink Triangle: The Nazi War Against Homosexuals.* 1986.

Religious Explorations

261.8 H7685-2 — *Homosexuality and Religion.* 1990.

261.8 M169-1 — McNeill, John. *Taking a Chance on God: Liberating Theology for Gays, Lesbians & Their Lovers, Families, & Friends.* 1988.

289.9M45 P466-1 — Perry, Troy. *Don't Be Afraid Anymore: The Story of Rev. Troy Perry.* 1990.

TELL ME

Why should it be my loneliness,
Why should it be my song,
Why should it be my dream,
deferred
overlong?

Langston Hughes

A Selected Bibliography for
*Lesbian and Gay
History Month*

June 1991

Los Angeles Public Library

WORLD AIDS DAY

December 1, 1991

616.97 B636-1 — Blake, Jeanne. *Risky Times: How To Be AIDS Smart.* Workman, 1990.

616.97 N933 — Nourse, Alan. *AIDS.* Watts, 1986.

616.97 H994 1987 — Hyde, Margaret and Elizabeth Forsyth. *AIDS: What Does It Mean To You?* Walker, 1987.

616.97 M376 — Martelli, Leonard. *When Someone You Know Has AIDS.* Cry, 1987.

616.97 A2885-14 — *AIDS, A Self-Care Manual.* IBS Press, 1989.

616.97 P351 — Peabody, Barbara. *Screaming Room.* Oak Tree Publications, 1986.

616.97 A2885-20 — *AIDS Information Sourcebook.* Oryx Press, 1989.

616.97 M742 — Monette, Paul. *Borrowed Time.* Harcourt Brace, 1988.

616.97 S556 — Shilts, Randy. *And The Band Played On.* St. Martin's, 1987.

616.97 N894 — Norwood, Chris. *Advice For Life.* Pantheon, 1987.

Los Angeles Public Library

Los Angeles Public Library/
Girl Scouts of Greater Los Angeles
patch, 2019
Institutional Archive,
Special Collections

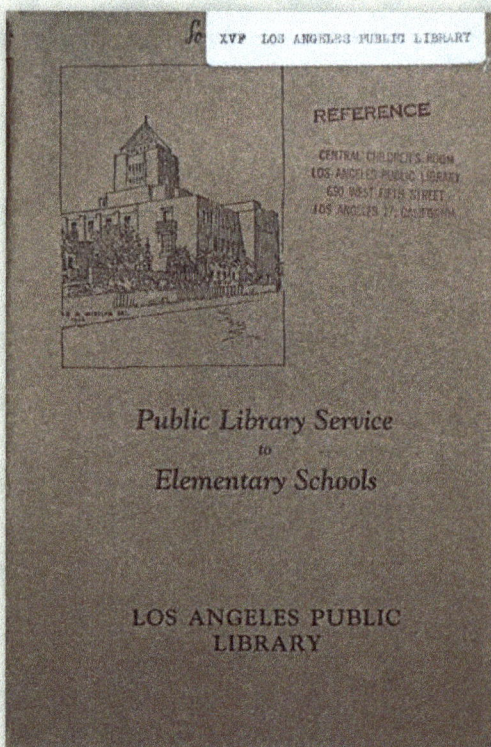

LEFT: Public Library Service to
Elementary Schools, 1926
Institutional Archive,
Special Collections

RIGHT AND OPPOSITE: Readers advisory
lists for youths, various
Institutional Archive,
Special Collections

Youth Services

Youth Services, encompassing both children and teens, has long been a central focus of the Library system. In its earliest days, the Library provided books for the fledgling Los Angeles school district, which would serve as a model for the branch system. From the Library's beginning until now, librarians have visited schools to introduce children to Library resources. Lists of picture and chapter books are constantly updated, and innovative services and programs are a mainstay of Library outreach. The Library has also pioneered special places, such as Student Zones and Teen'Scape, as well as fully developed Teen Web and Kids Path, to make the library available to Angeleno youth at all times.

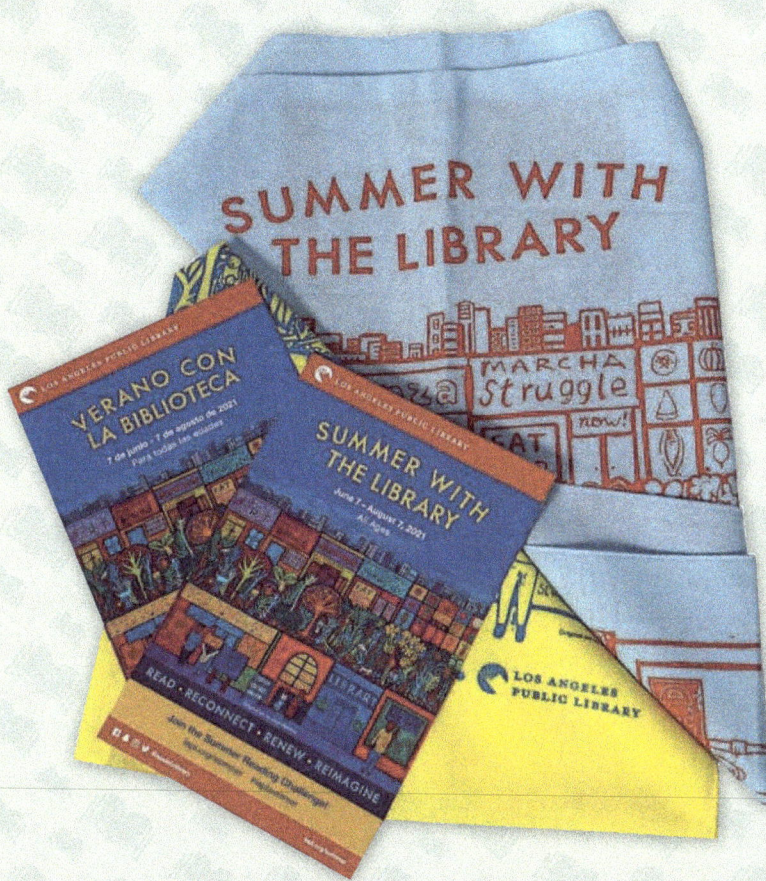

Summer Reading
materials, various
Courtesy of the Youth
Services Department

libros
divertidos
para
niños

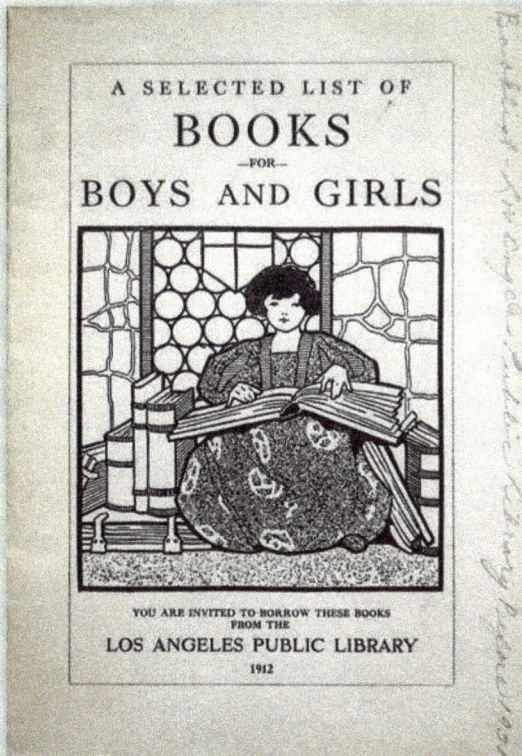

A SELECTED LIST OF
BOOKS
—FOR—
BOYS AND GIRLS

YOU ARE INVITED TO BORROW THESE BOOKS
FROM THE
LOS ANGELES PUBLIC LIBRARY
1912

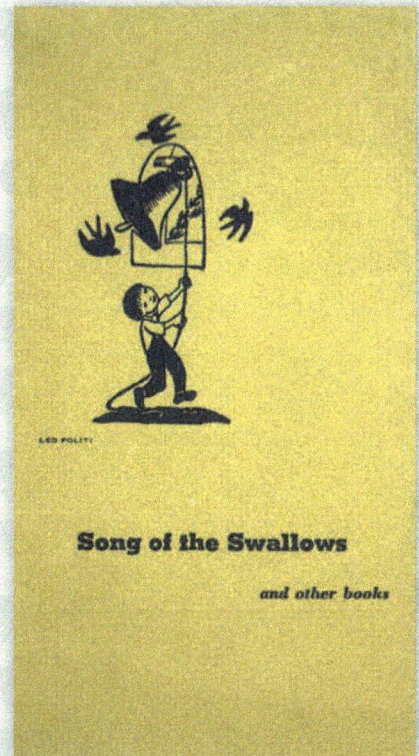

Song of the Swallows
and other books

Handouts relating to the GAB (Grandparents and Books) volunteer program, undated
Institutional Archive, Special Collections

Aprons for the STAR (Story Time and Reading) volunteer program, 2022
Courtesy of the Youth Services Department

A Library for the Future

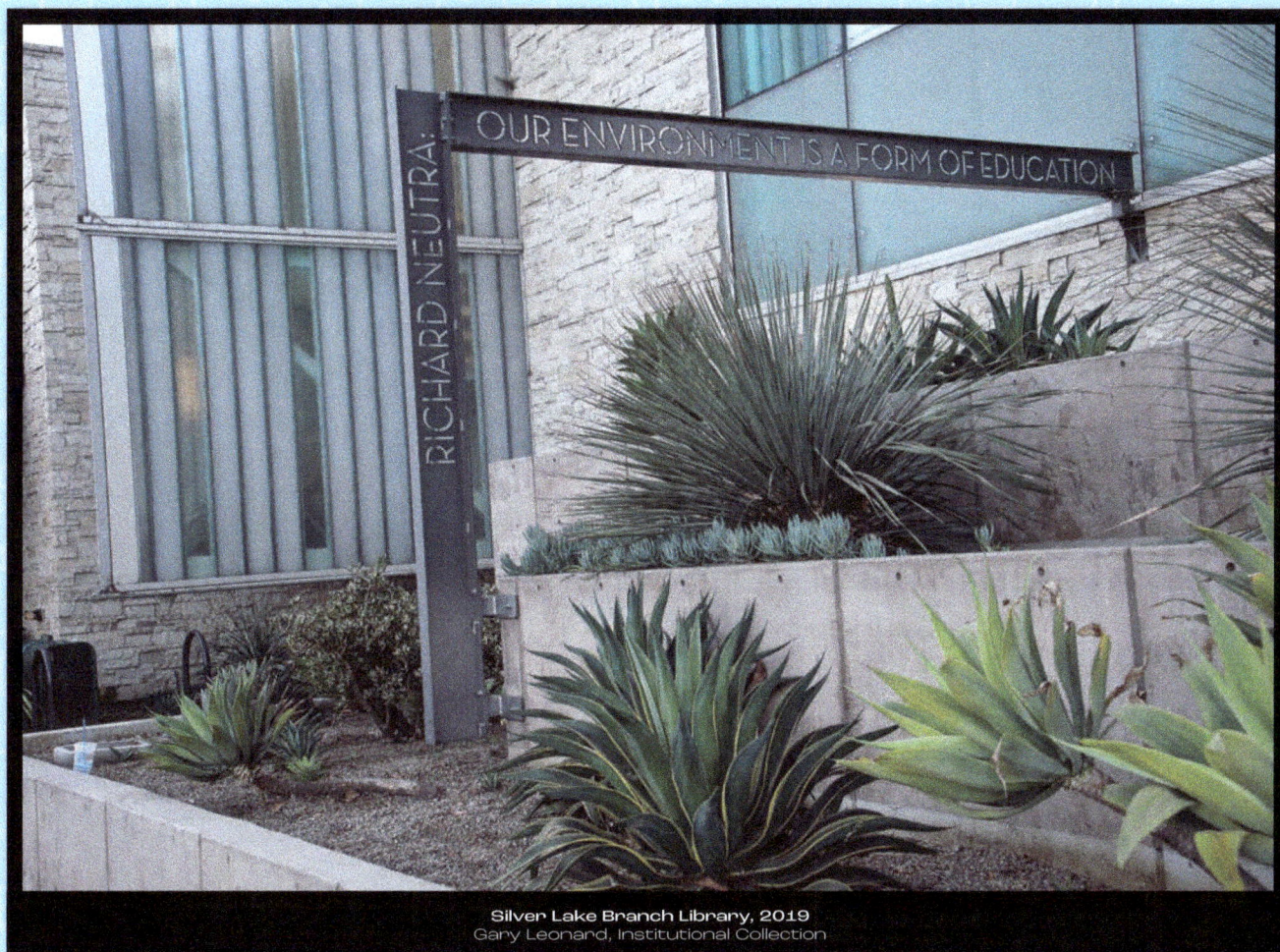

RICHARD NEUTRA:

OUR ENVIRONMENT IS A FORM OF EDUCATION

Silver Lake Branch Library, 2019
Gary Leonard, Institutional Collection

Another focus of the Library is sustainability, in which it continues to adopt innovations. The newest branches are eco-friendly, LEED-certified Gold Standard buildings that are part of the City of L.A.'s Sustainable Design Implementation Program, which offers more water efficiency, recycled materials and a low carbon footprint.

Octavia Lab at Central Library, 2019
Courtesy of the Los Angeles Public Library

Los Angeles Public Library supports creativity in the community with makerspaces, such as the award-winning Octavia Lab, which gives library cardholders free and unlimited access to state-of-the-art DIY design, fabrication, preservation, and story-telling technologies.

Girl Scout Troop 2291 learn about the library's E-services, 2019
Gary Leonard, Institutional Collection

A modern take on "The Traveling Branch," the Library's website provides resources to patrons anytime, anywhere, and enjoys over eleven million annual website visits. It includes a wide variety of e-media for streaming or downloading, such as e-books, audiobooks, videos, music, periodicals, and podcasts, as well as databases, catalogs, classes, videos, ESL, crafts, and other resources which empower patrons with the tools for life-long learning. The Library continues digitizing its special collections, available through the Tessa platform, to ensure easier public access to its photo collection, maps, and other significant images of Los Angeles history and culture.

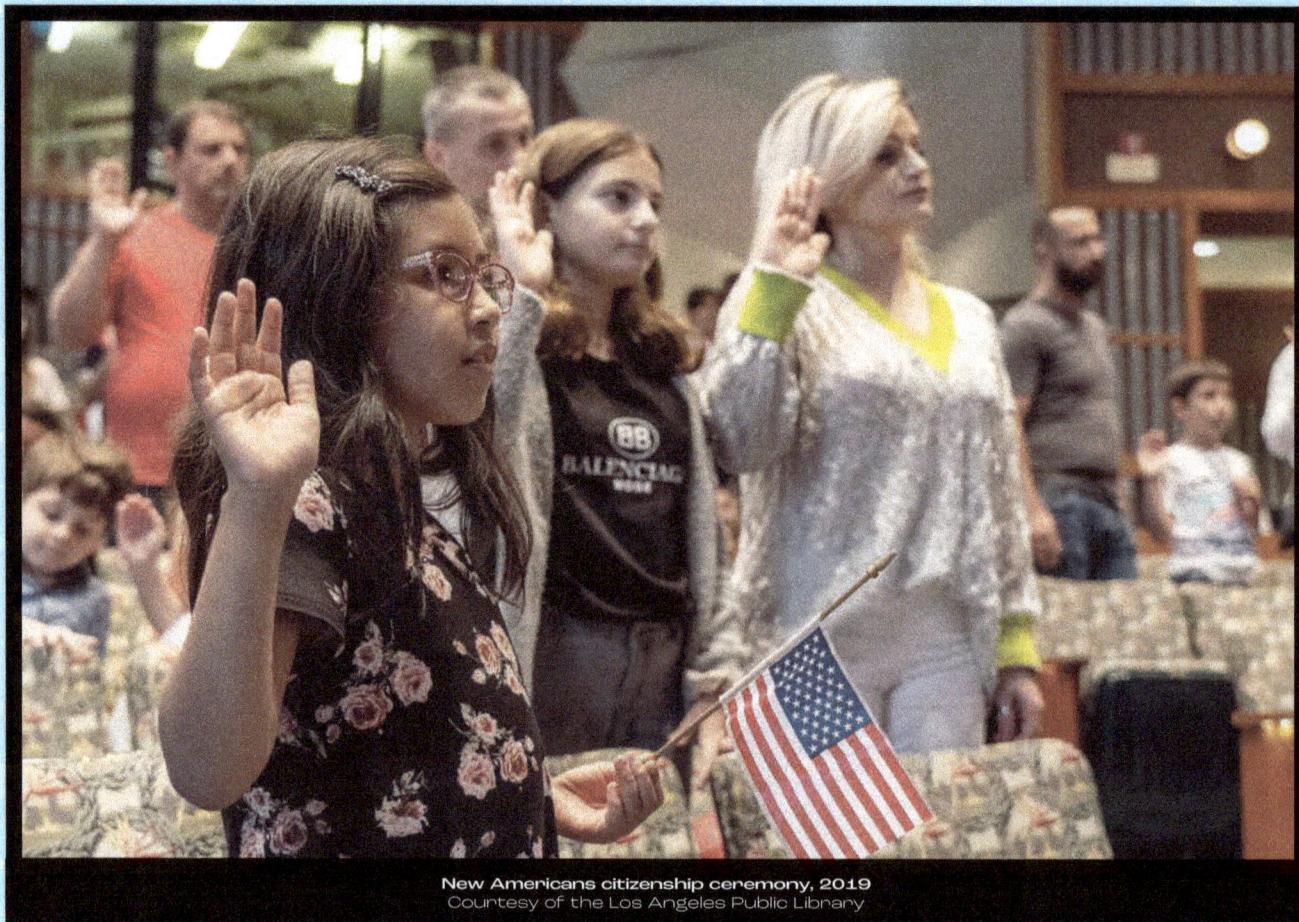
New Americans citizenship ceremony, 2019
Courtesy of the Los Angeles Public Library

Since 2012, more than 78,313 people have participated in the Library's New American services, which offers programs ranging from attending Citizenship classes to assistance in obtaining their Citizenship and many other needed immigration services. Through the Career Online High School initiative, the Library is also the first public library in the nation to offer an accredited online high school diploma for adults, and thus all of the opportunities which that provides. To date, 800 Angelenos have graduated through the program.

Career Online High School Graduates, 2018
Courtesy of the Los Angeles Public Library

Community Mobile Outreach unit, aka the Street Fleet, 2020
Courtesy of the Los Angeles Public Library

Los Angeles Public Library Outreach teams work with communities that are underserved or unconnected by delivering community-centered services, information, and technologies that entertain, enlighten and empower Angelenos of all ages and circumstances. Our Community Mobile Outreach unit, also known as the Street Fleet, meets people where they are and encourages library access by every Los Angeles resident.

NOTHING CAN KEEP US APART. *NOT EVEN LATE FEES* ♡

From February 1-14, return your overdue Los Angeles Public Library materials with no overdue fines.

#laplmissesyou

Book fine amnesty, 2016
Courtesy of the Los Angeles Public Library

Equitable access is also the hallmark of the Los Angeles Public Library's decision in 2020 to stop charging late fees for past-due books and other materials, which have historically had a disproportionate effect on families and individuals with limited resources. This action has helped the Library in fulfilling its mission to provide free and easy access to information, ideas, books and technology that enrich, educate and empower every individual in our city's diverse communities.

Where the Wild Things Are Puppets by Carol Onofrio, undated
Children's Literature Department

Established in 1979 by a dedicated group of twenty volunteers, the Friends of Children and Literature (FOCAL) brings children, books and authors together through special events and programs at the Central Library.

In 1980, FOCAL unanimously bestowed its first award upon Leo Politi, the distinguished author, illustrator, and Angeleno. The award was an original handmade puppet of the main character from his award-winning book, *Pedro: The Angel of Olvera Street*. FOCAL has continued the tradition with a unique puppet for its lucky winners.

Friends Groups

Friends of the Library are groups of volunteers who support the Los Angeles Public Library by providing program support to enhance the library services of a branch, department or special service. Friends also advocate for the financial support of the library and annually give thousands of dollars to branch libraries and Central Library departments. The Library is honored to have more than sixty active Friends of the Library groups.

Photo Friends handout for *Valley Times* image archive fundraising, 2013
Institutional Archive, Special Collections

Flyer for library program sponsored by the Friends of the North Hollywood Regional Branch Library, 1997
California Index

Friends of the Watts Branch Library membership form, 1989
California Index

BEST Friends

6 January 1989

Dear Friend:

Your assistance is needed as part of an effort to help the Los Angeles Public Library prepare for reopening this Spring.

In advance of the reopening, 1.8 million books are in need of processing.

BEST Friends is a non-profit organization, which supports the Central Library's Business/Economics and Science/Technology/Patents Departments. As many of you are affiliated with the business community, your help is very important.

Although the Library requests volunteers through March 1989, BEST Friends endorses the following dates:

  January 14, 1989 (Saturday)   9:00 A.M. through 5:30 P.M.
    (four hour shifts preferred)
  January 15, 1989 (Sunday)   1:00 P.M. through 5:00 P.M.
The above dates are designated for the Business and Economics Dept.

  January 28, 1989 (Saturday)   9:00 A.M. through 5:30 P.M.
    (four hour shifts preferred)
  January 29, 1989 (Sunday)   1:00 P.M. through 5:00 P.M.
The above dates are designated for the Science/Technology/Patents Dept.

The new location of the Central Branch of the Library is at 433 South Spring Street. (The building is the old Design Center) On site parking is free at the Center.

If you can spare some time, kindly call the Volunteer Hot Line at (213) 612-3261.

Thank you for your friendship and concern for the future of our Library.

Attached please find more information regarding this cause.

Sincerely yours,

Mignon Veasley
President
BEST Friends
(213) 236-3515

BUSINESS/ECONOMICS/SCIENCE/TECHNOLOGY Departments Los Angeles Public Library/Central Library
Post Office Box 71731 Los Angeles California 90071

BEST Friends appeal for business community volunteers
to move the Central Library collection to the temporary
Spring Street location, 1989
Anderson Collection

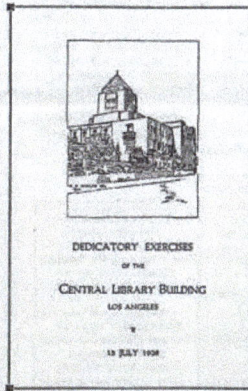

The Newsletter of the LAPL Central Library Docents

The Normal Hill News
Vol 5 • No. 4   August 1998

Looking Back

The new Central Library, what we call the Goodhue Building, had its official dedication on July 15, 1926. The culmination of years of planning and hard work, it was presented to the people of Los Angeles with great pride. Althea Warren, then a new member of LAPL, and later to become City Librarian following Everett Perry's unexpected death, was there and recalled the day in a article in the May, 1947 Broadcaster.

On July 15, 1926, the dedicatory exercises of our long-longed-for Central Library were held in the rotunda. A tan pamphlet printed in brown contains the eight contributions to the program. The Cornwell murals had not been completed so that the vaulted space was like the flat dish of lotus (big cream-colored, pink, and pale blue blossoms with quivering centers) from the Los Angeles County Public Library which delighted the History Department (then the Reference Room.)

It was a glorious midsummer's day, perhaps a little warm around the edges by mid-afternoon when the crowds had assembled. The speakers were seated behind the Registration counter. Bishop Johnson in his Episcopal robes gave the invocation. Then Mr. Carleton Monroe Winslow, who had superintended the completion of the building after Mr. Goodhue's death, paid tribute to the large group of superintendents, overseers, workmen, artists, engineers, and gardeners who had finished the work which Mr. Goodhue had to leave in April, 1924. Mr. Orra Monnette, President of the Library Board, accepted the library from its builders in an expansive address and turned it over to Councilman Boyle Workman, *See "Dedication," p.7*

DEDICATORY EXERCISES
OF THE
CENTRAL LIBRARY BUILDING
LOS ANGELES

15 JULY 1926

The program from Central's 1926 dedication. Read the text of Everett Perry's speech on page 7.

Normal Hill News, Newsletter of the
LAPL Central Library Docents
Special Collections

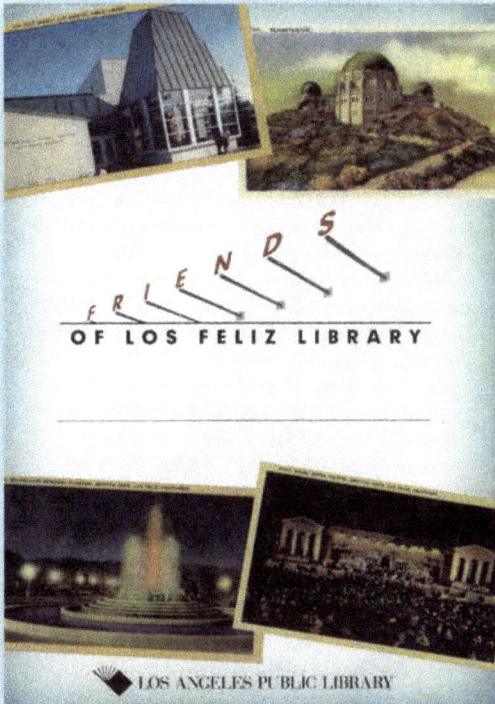

Friends of Los Feliz
bookplate, undated
Courtesy of the Los Feliz
Branch Library

VOLUNTEER!

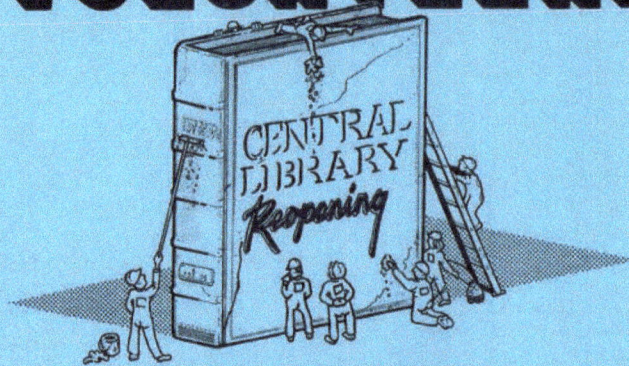

Help Prepare Books for the Central Library Reopening.

Closed by two arson fires, the Central Library is undergoing a $152.4 million renovation and expansion, to be completed in 1992.

Until then, the Central Library will move to temporary quarters opening in early 1989 at 433 S. Spring Street in downtown Los Angeles.

Your help is needed to:
■ Clean and inventory 700,000 water-damaged books
■ Shelve over 1.8 million books

Volunteer for day and evening shifts Monday through Saturday at the temporary site. Free parking.

FOR INFORMATION CALL (213) 612-3261

L O S A N G E L E S P U B L I C L I B R A R Y

Call for volunteers to shelve books at Central Library, 1988
Institutional Archive, Special Collections

Library Adult Reading Project
TUTOR CERTIFICATE

CALIFORNIA LITERACY CAMPAIGN

_____ has satisfactorily completed literacy training conducted by the Library Adult Reading Project and is certified to tutor adults in reading and writing English.

Los Angeles Public Library
Library Adult Reading Project
1636 W. Manchester Avenue
Los Angeles, CA 90047

Trainer _____

Project Director _____

Funded by California Library Services Act, Special Services

Library Adult Reading Project tutor certificate, circa 1990
Institutional Archive, Special Collections

Library Volunteers

During tough times and good times, volunteers have long been integral to the public services of the Library, demonstrating a strong and abiding connection between the Library and the community. Volunteers have assisted in library programs and community activities, as well as helping the Library recover from earthquakes, fires, and relocations that have occurred during the institution's long history.

Call for volunteers for Service to Shut-ins program, undated
Institutional Archive, Special Collections

Branded library book,
Literature & Fiction Department

Replica library brand, 2023
Courtesy of Photo Friends

Following the example of mission and convent libraries, Charles Lummis, City Librarian from 1905-10, designed a library brand with the aim of marking valuable titles from the historic Californian and Southwest collection to keep them from being rustled by book thieves. Rare book librarian and historian John Bruckman claimed no branded book was ever stolen. The brand itself was not so lucky, disappearing from the library collection and leaving behind only rumors of where it might have strayed. The brand displayed here is a reproduction.

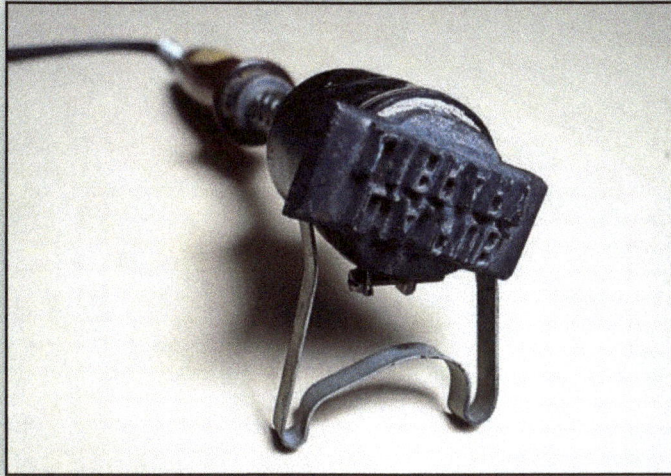

Los Angeles Public Library electric brand, undated
Institutional Archive, Special Collections

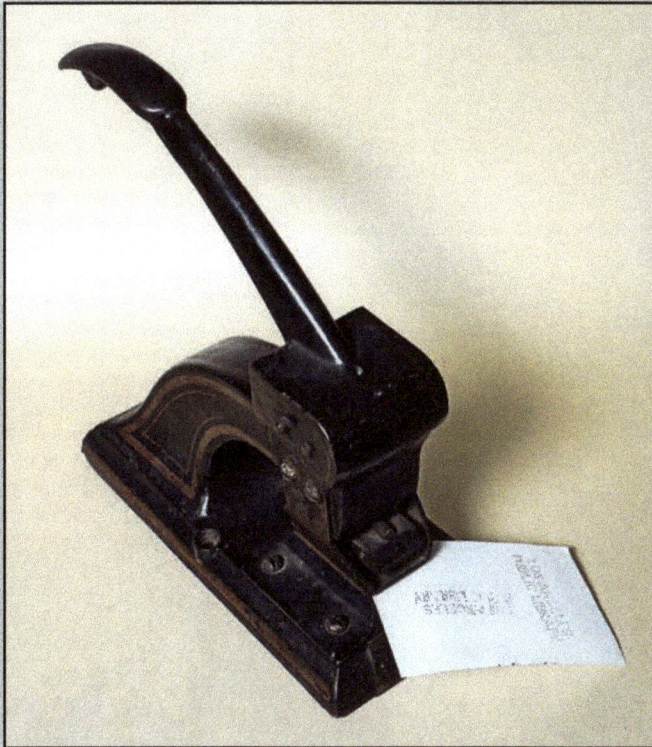

Los Angeles Public Library perforator
with book example, undated
Institutional Archive, Special Collections

Making a Mark

The oldest examples of ownership marks are older than books, stretching back to the tablets of Ancient Egypt circa 1300 BCE. While ink stamps have long been the mainstay of stained-fingered librarians, other more emphatic methods of establishing ownership have been employed, notably perforation of pages, branding the "heads" (the top edge) and embossing seals. Here are examples used in our history.

Library Foundation of Los Angeles

Founded in 1992 in response to the successful Save the Books campaign for Central Library, the Library Foundation of Los Angeles (LFLA) is a private nonprofit that provides critical support to the Los Angeles Public Library system resulting in free programs, resources, and services available to the millions of adults, children, and youth of Los Angeles. The popular ALOUD cultural programming series has been a hallmark for over two decades, and in 2022, the Foundation launched a Creators in Residence program designed to engage creative Angelenos from a multitude of disciplines. Consider becoming an LFLA member today!

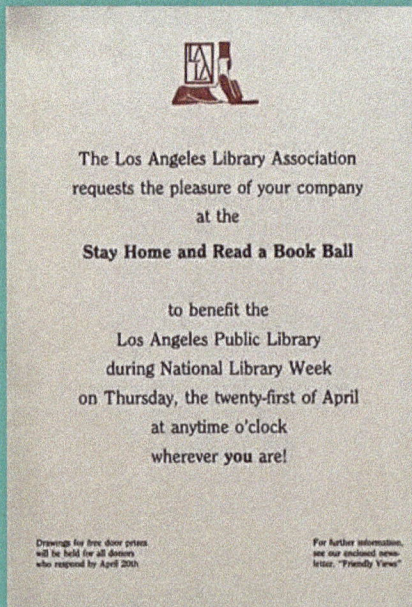

The Los Angeles Library Association requests the pleasure of your company at the

Stay Home and Read a Book Ball

to benefit the Los Angeles Public Library during National Library Week on Thursday, the twenty-first of April at anytime o'clock wherever **you** are!

Drawings for free door prizes will be held for all donors who respond by April 20th.

For further information, see our enclosed newsletter, "Friendly Views."

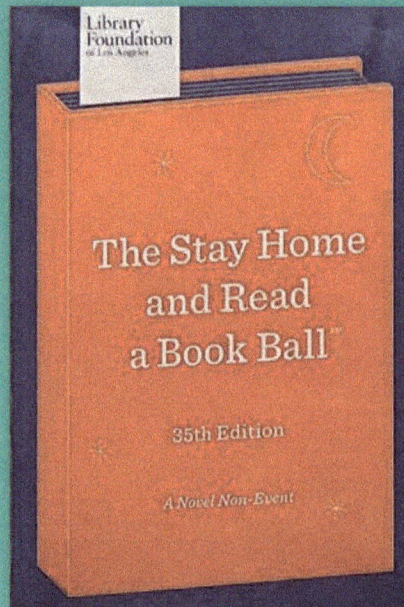

The Stay Home and Read a Book Ball™

35th Edition

A Novel Non-Event

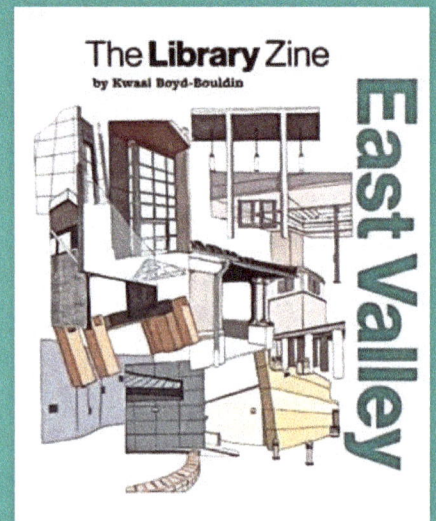

The **Library** Zine
by Kwasi Boyd-Bouldin

East Valley

ABOVE LEFT AND RIGHT:
Stay Home and Read a Book Ball Invitations, 1988 & 2023
Anderson Collection & Courtesy of the Library Foundation of Los Angeles

Started by the Library Association of Los Angeles (LALA), a predecessor to the Library Foundation, the annual Stay Home and Read a Book Ball is a popular "non-event" that encourages residents to support the Library Foundation by making a donation and curling up at home with their favorite book on a designated day.

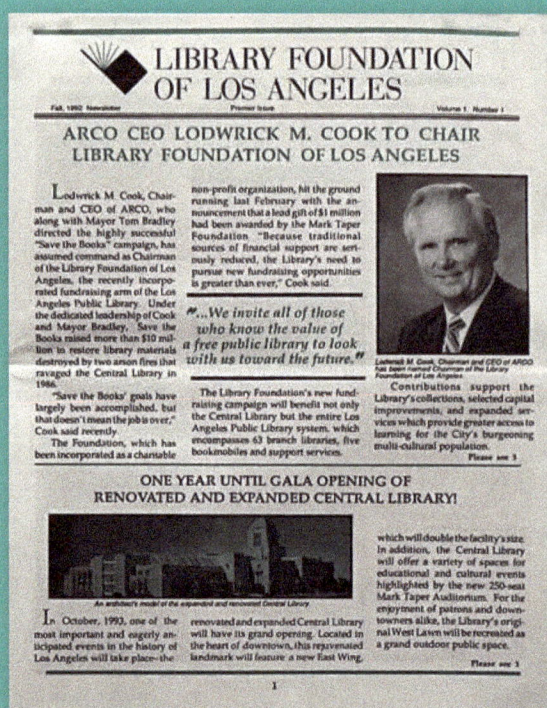

LIBRARY FOUNDATION OF LOS ANGELES

Fall, 1992 Newsletter · Premier Issue · Volume 1, Number 1

ARCO CEO LODWRICK M. COOK TO CHAIR LIBRARY FOUNDATION OF LOS ANGELES

Lodwrick M. Cook, Chairman and CEO of ARCO, who along with Mayor Tom Bradley directed the highly successful "Save the Books" campaign, has assumed command as Chairman of the Library Foundation of Los Angeles, the recently incorporated fundraising arm of the Los Angeles Public Library. Under the dedicated leadership of Cook and Mayor Bradley, Save the Books raised more than $10 million to restore library materials destroyed by two arson fires that ravaged the Central Library in 1986.

"Save the Books' goals have largely been accomplished, but that doesn't mean the job is over," Cook said recently.

The Foundation, which has been incorporated as a charitable non-profit organization, hit the ground running last February with the announcement that a lead gift of $1 million had been awarded by the Mark Taper Foundation. "Because traditional sources of financial support are seriously reduced, the Library's need to pursue new fundraising opportunities is greater than ever," Cook said.

"...We invite all of those who know the value of a free public library to look with us toward the future."

Lodwrick M. Cook, Chairman and CEO of ARCO, has been named Chairman of the Library Foundation of Los Angeles.

The Library Foundation's new fundraising campaign will benefit not only the Central Library but the entire Los Angeles Public Library system, which encompasses 63 branch libraries, five bookmobiles and support services.

Contributions support the Library's collections, selected capital improvements, and expanded services which provide greater access to learning for the City's burgeoning multi-cultural population.

Please see 3

ONE YEAR UNTIL GALA OPENING OF RENOVATED AND EXPANDED CENTRAL LIBRARY!

An architect's model of the expanded and renovated Central Library.

In October, 1993, one of the most important and eagerly anticipated events in the history of Los Angeles will take place—the renovated and expanded Central Library will have its grand opening. Located in the heart of downtown, this rejuvenated landmark will feature a new East Wing, which will double the facility's size. In addition, the Central Library will offer a variety of spaces for educational and cultural events highlighted by the new 250-seat Mark Taper Auditorium. For the enjoyment of patrons and downtowners alike, the Library's original West Lawn will be recreated as a grand outdoor public space.

Please see 5

1

RIGHT: Premier Issue of the Library Foundation of Los Angeles Newsletter, 1992
Anderson Collection

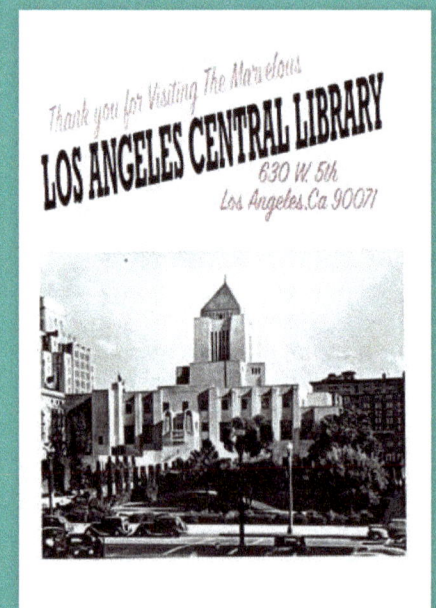

Thank you for Visiting The Marvelous
LOS ANGELES CENTRAL LIBRARY
630 W. 5th
Los Angeles, Ca 90071

ABOVE: Creators in Residence Zines by Kwasi Boyd-Bouldin and River Garza, 2022
Courtesy of the Library Foundation of Los Angeles

Acknowledgments

Jim and Christina would like to thank the following people for their assistance and support with **LAPL150— Our Story Is Yours.**

The exhibition (and all of the LAPL150 celebration!) is the brainchild of mad genius Diane Olivio-Posner, ably assisted by Kevin Awakuni and Steve Orozco. *LAPL150: Our Story Is Yours* was beautifully designed by Amy Inouye, and supported by Photo Friends (special thanks for the Brand!). The exhibition was realized by Mitch Browning, without whom it would not have happened, and installed by Brian DeMaree and Victor Olivares. Todd Lerew of the Library Foundation was very kind to lend his expertise and equipment for the exhibition's audiovisual elements, and Benjamin Roncal was also key to that process.

Keith Kesler made promotion of the exhibition a whole lot of fun, and did a stellar job with producing, directing, and editing the short documentary about the fire at the Hollywood Branch Library. Library historians Tiffney Sanford and Kelly Wallace were essential in telling that chapter of the LAPL story.

Christine Adolph deserves special thanks for her archival feats in winnowing out exceptional photos of LAPL's history.

The Digitization & Special Collections department was a crucial and enthusiastic collaborator on *LAPL150: Our Story Is Yours*, particularly Rose Knopka, with assists from Sung Kim, Dan Nishimoto, Juan Avalos, and Ryan Peña. Their provision of founding historical documents, ephemera, and wonderful surprises like the original watercolor renderings of branch libraries, was directly responsible for imbuing the exhibition with a sense of living history. Thank you!

Many thanks to Ani Boyadjian for the strong support (organizational and otherwise) of the project, from the beginning to even after the end. The title "Our Story Is Yours" was a wonderful gift from Christa Dietrick. Thank you, Bob Anderson and Susan Lendroth, for their generosity (and quick turnaround!) in editing the text copy. We are thankful for the content assists from Nick Beyelia, Sye Gutierrez, and Ziba Zehdar. Ricardo Ortiz was very helpful in our visits to off-site storage at Anderson Street warehouse, where we found many historical documents that made their way into the exhibition cases (and many more forgotten treasures that we wish we had the scope to feature).

Fact-checking assistance came from LAPL historians Robin Myers (for recent history) and Jeffrey Nelson (for early history). Joyce Cooper and Helen Neal were instrumental in their support of branch history research. Other essential system history was provided by Bob Anderson, Peter Persic, Roy Stone, Judy Ostrander, and the work of the late Glenna Dunning. A special thanks goes to Pearl Yonezawa for her donation of historical material, some of which originally was preserved by LAPL legend Helene Mochedlover, may she rest in peace.

A big thanks is owed, not only by us but by anyone interested in LAPL history, to Raquel Borden from the office of Board of Library Commissioners for her commitment to preserving the primary documents of the Library's history, growth, and governance. We are grateful for her institutional knowledge and for the Board's donation of the historical embosser.

Thank you to Library Administration, including John F. Szabo, City Librarian, Susan Broman, Assistant City Librarian, Kren Malone, Central Library Director, and Ana Campos, Assistant Central Library Director.

A deeply held thanks goes to the Photo Collection Staff: Valeria Barragan, Terri Garst, Wendy Horowitz, and Fernando Sauceda. A special thank you for your daily work that keeps *LAPL150: Our Story Is Yours* looking good!

But the biggest thanks is reserved for all of our colleagues at LAPL, past and present, who have dedicated themselves to making the history of the Los Angeles Public Library a story worth celebrating. Thank you, Los Angeles Public Library!

About the Authors

James Sherman began his career with the Los Angeles Public Library in 2005 and has been a Reference Librarian in the Literature & Fiction Department since 2006. He has an MLIS from San Jose State University, an MFA in Theater, Film, & Television from UCLA, and a BA in History from Columbia University. He both edited and contributed to the publication *Feels Like Home: Reflections on Central Library* (Photo Friends Publications, 2018). His daughters, Isabel and Lillian, think he's fairly cool most of the time.

Christina Rice began her career with the Los Angeles Public Library in 2005 and has been the Senior Librarian of the library's historic photo collection since 2009. She has curated multiple library exhibitions including *Life on a String: The Yale Puppeteers and the Turnabout Theatre* (2021). She is the author of *Mean... Moody...Magnificent! Jane Russell and the Marketing of a Hollywood Legend* (University Press of Kentucky, 2021) and *Ann Dvorak Hollywood's Forgotten Rebel* (University Press of Kentucky, 2013). She proudly resides in the San Fernando Valley with her husband, writer Joshua Hale Fialkov, their daughter Gable, and two dogs who are often irritating but always adorable.

LAPL 150—Our Story Is Yours: A Los Angeles Public Library Sesquicentennial Celebration
Exhibition and Book Curated by James Sherman, Librarian, Literature & Fiction Department
and Christina Rice, Senior Librarian, Photo Collection
Text © 2023 James Sherman
Images © 2023 Los Angeles Public Library

This book was published in conjunction with the exhibition at Los Angeles Central Library, 2023.

Published by:
Los Angeles Public Library
630 W. Fifth Street, Los Angeles CA 90071

ISBN-13: 978-1-7346713-8-4 (hardcover print)

Printed in the United States

Exhibition and Book Designed by Amy Inouye, Future Studio Los Angeles

Cover collage by Christina Rice

LOS ANGELES PUBLIC LIBRARY

www.ingramcontent.com/pod-product-compliance
Lightning Source LLC
Chambersburg PA
CBHW040318100426
42811CB00012B/1476